SILV
THREADS
A LOOK AT PAISLEY'S PAST

DAVID ROWAND
Fellow, University of Paisley. F.S.A. Scot.

Paslet Publications

SILVER THREADS
A LOOK AT PAISLEY'S PAST
© David Rowand 2000

First published in 2000 by
PASLET PUBLICATIONS,
8a Calside Avenue, Paisley,
Scotland, PA2 6DD.

Visit our website-
www.pasletpublications.btinternet.co.uk
e-mail:pasletpublications@hotmail.com

Printed in Scotland by Bell & Bain Ltd, Glasgow.
Design & Layout by Chris Rowand.

ISBN No. 0 9539599 0 2
British Library Cataloguing in Publication Data.
A CIP record for this book is available from the
British Library.

Introduction

Over the last three years, the author produced a series of weekly articles which were published in the Paisley Daily Express. So popular were these little cameos of Paisley's history, that some of them were enshrined in a locally best-selling book, 'Golden Threads'.

This new book, 'Silver Threads', is the sequel to 'Golden Threads'. The articles selected, highlight in detail various periods from Paisley's long and illustrious history.

'Silver Threads' is a book written by a true Paisley Buddie and dedicated to Paisley readers, both at home and abroad. Paisley folks take a deep interest in tales of their old town's past, and it is this I have tried to capture in the following pages.

It is said of Paisley folks that you cannot tell them much about their old town, they appear to know it all! Every Paisley household has a story to tell or a cherished old photograph to show. In the preparation of this book, my thanks go to the people of Paisley, who in their unstinted generosity have shared some of their 'Paisley treasures' with me, and helped make this book possible.

My thanks go the staff of Paisley Museum and Paisley Reference Library for the use of archive material. To Chris, my son, for his input as graphic artist, I give my thanks as a grateful father. To Mary, my wife, who carefully proof read the book with all the acumen of a schoolmistress, I tender my deep thanks.

David Rowand   Paisley, Scotland 2000

Contents

A Paisley Poem

Common Seal of the Burgh of Paisley showing three shields, with mitred abbot in centre holding a crosier. Last used officially in 1912.

Ring-a-ring, o' roses,
A pocketful of posies,
A-tishoo, a-tishoo,
We all fall down.

Most of us remember this wee poem from our childhood. In the school playground, we would form a circle, sing "A-tishoo, A-tishoo!" and fall to the ground. Little did we then realise how macabre the rhyme really was. It was, in fact, a description of the symptoms of the dreaded "Black Death", or bubonic plague. Rosy-red pustules would appear on the body. Bouts of sneezing followed. After this, you "fell down dead".

However, the Paisley version, adapted from this gruesome little poem, had nothing to do with the dreaded plague, despite the fact that Paisley had its first recorded outbreak in 1456 and its last in 1645.

Our local version, handed down over the generations and used as a playground game, read as follows:

A ring, a ring, o' roses,
A cup, a cup, a shell.
Maw's away to Hamilton,
Tae buy a new bell.
If you don't want it,
I'll get it for ma sel',
A ring, a ring, o' roses,
A cup, a cup, a shell.

The Paisley Penny of 1798 showing the old Paisley coat of arms.

The significance of the words becomes clear when we look at the picture of the old Paisley Coat of Arms, used by the Town Council until 1912.

"A ring" is worn on the hand of the central figure of the Abbot of Paisley Abbey, who received his insignia of Mitre and Ring in 1334, from Pope Benedict XII.

The "roses" appear at the top of the right hand shield. These were the red cinquefoils, symbols of the Hamilton family, who had a close association with

When the new Abbey Bridge was constructed in 1882, pride of place was given to Paisley's coat of arms. It is a beautiful example of cast-iron work by the local engineering firm Hanna, Donald and Wilson.

The old Paisley Burgh Crest with a mural crown depicting the shields with a shell, the roses and the cups.

Paisley Abbey. For example, Claud Hamilton, nephew of Paisley's last Abbot, inherited all the abbey lands and their revenues shortly after the Reformation.

"A cup" refers to the three covered cups in the lower shield. This was the emblem of Abbot George Schaw (1473-1498), who first raised Paisley from a village to a burgh in 1488.

"A shell" in the poem, refers to the single scallop shell on another of the shields. This was the mediaeval badge worn by pilgrims going to the shrine of St James of Compostella, in Spain. Significantly, he was the family patron saint of the High Stewards of Scotland, one of whom founded Paisley Abbey. St James was one of the saints to whom the abbey was dedicated. The scallop shell would also have been worn by mediaeval pilgrims attending the shrine of our local holy man, Saint Mirin.

"Maw's away to Hamilton,
To buy a new bell,"

Unlike the Arms of the City of Glasgow, no bell appears on Paisley's Coat of Arms. So what is the connection with the poem? The bell was the Paisley "Silver Bells".This was a prize first presented in 1620, by the previously mentioned Hamilton family, the Earls of Abercorn, to the winning horse at the Paisley Races.

Until 1907, the "Silver Bells" were proudly hung between the ears of winning horses at Paisley Racecourse. The "Silver Bells", one of Britain's oldest horse- racing prizes, are now on display in Paisley Museum.

The old coat of arms of Paisley and its motto "Let Paisley flourish, by the preaching of thy word", can still be seen on some of the town's older buildings.

As in the motto, the Paisley version of "Ring o' roses" has flourished over the centuries. Its words, which readers may remember from childhood, can still be heard, on occasion, in local school playgrounds.

The Paisley Silver Bells, first used as a horse-racing prize in 1620,
now to be seen in Paisley Museum. (photo : courtesy Paisley Museum)

7

The ill-fated Jean Cochrane

Jean Cochrane (1662-1695).
A Paisley girl who married "Bonnie Dundee".

In the 17th Century, Paisley had its own Romeo and Juliet. Their love story took place during a blood-soaked chapter in Scotland's history, when there were two factions in a struggle for religious freedom. The Episcopalians, who supported the established church ruled by the King and his bishops and the Covenanters who wanted freedom of worship, were bitter enemies.

John Graham of Claverhouse was a King's man. Known to his supporters as "Bonnie Dundee" and to his enemies, the Covenanters, as "Bloody Clavers", he met and fell in love with a Paisley girl called Jean Cochrane.

She was the third daughter of William Lord Cochrane, a strong supporter of the Covenanters, whose family home was in the Place of Paisley. Her grandfather, the Earl of Cassilis and her uncle, Cochrane of Ochiltree, were both leading Covenanters.

When her father died in 1679, Jean was taken to Edinburgh, where she met and fell in love with the handsome soldier, Colonel John Graham of Claverhouse. After a while, the couple decided to marry. Jean's mother was horrified. She hated Claverhouse and called him the "Persecutor" for his merciless slaughter of the Covenanters. The supporters of Claverhouse were equally worried. It was put about that "Claverhouse was more zealous in his attentions to the daughter of a religiously suspect family than he was pursuing rebels". However, love triumphed and, despite ill-feeling on both sides, the marriage was arranged. When Claverhouse and his troop of cavalry were billeted in the Place of Paisley, the Cochrane family home, the ceremony took place in Paisley Abbey on 10th June, 1684.

During the wedding reception, a message was brought to Claverhouse that a gathering of Covenanters was taking place in the district. He immediately changed into field service uniform, mounted his horse "Satan" and rode off with

"Bonnie Dundee", the handsome soldier, who married Jean Cochrane in Paisley Abbey on 10th June 1684. Not long after the wedding, he was killed at the battle of Killiecrankie, leaving Jean a widow.

his troops in search of the rebels. "There was never a more saddle-sore and weary bridegroom than Claverhouse when he dismounted three days later, on his return to Paisley to claim his bride".

One year later, Claverhouse was struck off the list of Privy Councillors as "having married into a fanatic family of the Cochranes, it was not considered safe to commit the King's secrets to him". However, the King, James II, forgave him and created him Viscount Dundee. Soon after this, Jean gave birth to a son, but her happiness was short-lived. Her husband was killed at the battle of Killiecrankie, fighting for the now exiled King James against the new King, William of Orange. Before the year was out, Jean's infant son was also dead.

A few years later, Jean married Colonel William Livingston, Viscount Kilsyth,

The coffin containing the bodies of Jean Cochrane and infant son as discovered in a vault, at Kilsyth Church, on 27th July 1795.

who had been one of her husband's officers. They decided to leave Scotland and settle in Holland where there was a large Scottish community. A son was born to them in 1695. That year, Jean, her husband, their young baby and the family maid were all staying at an old inn in Utrecht. Unknown to them, a large quantity of peat turves was stored in the loft above their living quarters. The turves were freshly cut and heavy with recent rain. Suddenly, "with no more warning than a loud crack," the floor of the loft above them gave way. Jean, her infant son and her faithful maid were killed. Her husband miraculously escaped injury.

The bodies of the tragic Jean and her child were carefully embalmed in Holland and eventually sent to Scotland. They were buried in the Kilsyth family vault in Kilsyth Church.

Jean's story, however, did not end there. In 1795, an Edinburgh newpaper reported an incident when some young people went down to visit the vault where she was buried and, "prompted by curiosity", tore open the lid of a lead coffin. They found two bodies, mother and child, in a remarkable state of preservation. The bodies were sketched and recorded before their re-interrment. When the church was demolished, the vault was filled in. In 1850, a large memorial was erected nearby, telling the story of their death. Like Shakespeare's Juliet, this young Paisley woman led an ill-starred life, which ended in tragedy.

The Place of Paisley, the family home of William Lord Cochrane, a strong supporter of the Covenanters. It was here that Jean, his third daughter, was raised.

Slezer's View of Paisley

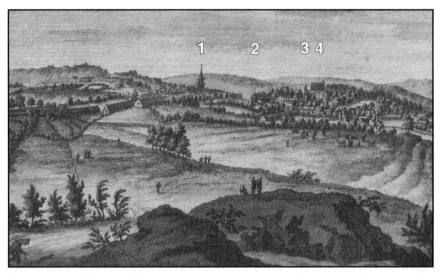

Slezer's view of Paisley. This original aquatint engraving from the author's collection was published in Amsterdam in 1707.The view shows 1 The Tollbooth. 2 The Bridge of Paisley. 3 Abbot Schaw's gatehouse tower. 4 The nave of Paisley Abbey.

The earliest known authentic view of Paisley appeared in a book called "Theatrium Scotiae". This beautifully illustrated book was first published in 1693 and contained engravings of the old historic towns of Scotland, such as Glasgow, Melrose, St Andrews and, of course, Paisley.

The man who illustrated the book was Captain John Slezer. This highly talented Dutch artist was Royal Engineer in Scotland under King Charles II. His view of Paisley was drawn about 1680, some thirteen years before it appeared in his book. Slezer chose as his vantage point Saucel Hill, the highest land nearest the town centre. His wonderful picture gives a panoramic view of the town as it stood at that time.

He shows the town of Paisley built from the top to the foot of gently swelling hills, from which the citizens could enjoy extensive views. A contemporary writer reported that, "Paisley has every advantage that can arise from a free circulation of air, while from the general declivity of the streets a ready descent is given to the waters, which on every shower that falls, washes them clean. All of this still further contributes to the salubrity of the town"!

In 1680, Paisley was, indeed, a healthy little town. Although it had been made a Burgh as far back as 1488, it had not grown greatly over the centuries. It was

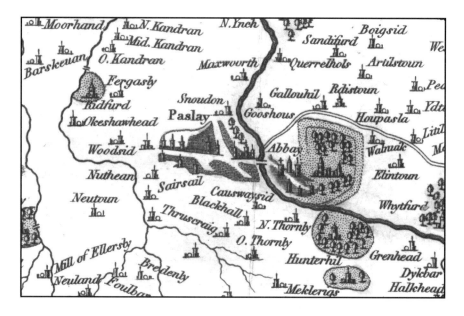

An extract from Blaeu's map of Renfrewshire dated 1654.
On one side of the River Cart, the Abbey appears surrounded by Abbot Schaw's great wall. The town of Paisley appears on the other with some old familiar place names.

still a small, rural, market village, clustering round its mediaeval streets and its remnant of an abbey. The town's narrow principal street, the High Street, only extended a half-mile. It contained a handful of well-built town houses or tenements, built in earlier days by the monastery and some of the leading county families of Renfrewshire.

In the centre of Slezer's picture rises the town's tollbooth steeple, the proud symbol of burgh status. It had been rebuilt in 1610 on its original site at the corner of Moss Street and High Street. An expensive new clock, which had been added to the tollbooth in 1647, was admired by visitors to the town.

At this time, Paisley only had one bridge crossing the River Cart. Slezer drew this as a single-arched structure to the right of the tollbooth. Before 1490, a bridge had existed at this point, connecting the abbey with its little satellite village of Paisley. The abbey and the village had grown up in tandem. The bridge was rebuilt about 1586, complete with a custom booth or town's port. It became known as the Bridge of Paisley. Today, St James Bridge next to the Town Hall occupies the same site.

In Slezer's time, the River Cart was a pure and limpid river with salmon and trout abounding in its clear waters. The reaches of the river above the Hammills contained fresh-water pearls. The Paisley pearls grew in abundance and were so fine that they were compared favourably with the best Oriental pearls. The reputation of Paisley's fine pearls was noted throughout Europe. Even the famous French jeweller Tavernier gave high praise of them. For any Buddies out there wishing to make their fortune by pearl-fishing, don't bother, the pearls are long gone!

On the right of the bridge, Slezer drew a cluster of little buildings huddled round what remained of Paisley Abbey. The abbey's mediaeval nave towers above its surroundings. Note there is no central tower, as it had collapsed around 1560. The only tower shown immediately to the left of the abbey is Abbot Schaw's great gatehouse tower. Only the skeleton of the south transept wall is recorded, together with St Mirin's Chapel. Paisley Abbey's mediaeval nave, at that time, was the only established church in town. Hints of what may be older outbuildings of the abbey lie next to the river bank. A remnant of the old, mediaeval abbey boundary wall, built by Abbot Schaw in 1485, is just barely visible skirting the river bank.

Slezer shows Causeyside as a row of single-storey, but-and-ben type cottages running from the middle left of the picture down in the direction of the tollbooth. The roofs of these humble little dwellings were thatched in straw or heather with turves for the ridges of the roofs. From a tax imposed by the Scot's Parliament in 1695 called the Poll Tax Roll, made only two years after Slezer's book was published, we learn that Paisley had 460 houses and a population of just over 1000 people over the age of sixteen. Of these 66 were employed as weavers, with a further 33 weavers in the surrounding districts. The high number employed in this business suggests that, even then, Paisley was a thriving centre of the textile trade. At this time, Paisley was also a centre of shoemaking employing 33 sons of St Mirin and St Crispin. Paisley, in these days, was "a very pleasant and well built little town, plentifully provided with all sorts of grain, fruits, coals, peats, fishes and what else is proper for the comfortable use of man, or can be expected in any other place in the kingdom."

Slezer's view of Paisley was republished and re-engraved several times. In some cases, birds were added to the sky, trees to the foreground and cattle to the fields, all under the name of artistic license.

Years later, one of Paisley's poets must have stood on the same spot as Slezer to compose these lines:

The bonnie toun O Paisley,
Stands upon three hills,
And thro' them runs the River Cart,
That caws the Seedhill Mill.

Gordon's Loan - the legend

Looking down Gordon Street towards Lonend in 1920. On the left, a group of schoolchildren stand in front of the old fire station. Notice the boy pushing a large handbarrow. On the right, next to the elegant 'Paisley standard' street lamp, are the brick offices of James Paton, colour printers. Beyond, the row of ruined old weavers' cottages run down to Lonend. The large chimney at the bottom of the street formed part of the boiler house serving the old fever hospital at Bladda. This brick building also served as a 'British Restaurant' during WWII.(photo :courtesy D.Malcolm)

In the palmy days of the weaving trade, Gordon's Loan was noted as a street full of hand loom weavers. Weaving cotton goods was their speciality. Almost every weaver in this street was Radical to a man, both in politics and religion. Despite being relatively poor compared to the higher paid silk weavers, this group of men boasted that they formed the "aristocracy of Paisley intellect!"

In their high-flown claim, they even gave the name of their street a classical one. They called Gordon's Loan the "Grecian Bend". The adopted name, however fanciful, was fairly appropriate, as Gordon's Loan did run in a gentle curve between Lonend and Causeyside.

One of the intellectual weavers, who had been brought up in this street from early boyhood and who, indeed, became a published author, was David Gilmour.

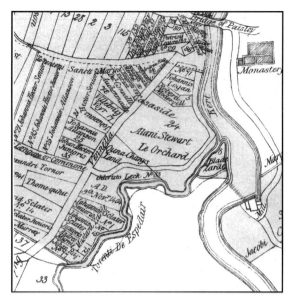

An extract of a conjectural map of Paisley between 1490-1545, showing Gordon's Loan appearing beneath the orchard belonging to Alan Stewart.

When he published his reminiscences of Gordon's Loan, one local historian asked him if he knew how the street first got its name. Gilmour apologised for such a glaring omission in his book and came up with the following story, which he said had been handed down through the generations.

In mediaeval times, two brothers called Gordon who had travelled from England on a pilgrimage, presented themselves at the gate of Paisley Abbey. As pilgrims they requested admittance and shelter within the abbey, but were refused admittance until they served a penance for their past sins. Part of the penance was "to live under the earth beyond the reach of the sun's rays until their hearts were touched by the inner light of the holy mother church". The brothers set out to fulfill their penance by digging a cave in the middle of the bend in what later became Gordon's Loan. The cave was situated near a holy shrine and within the sound of its consecrated bell. During this time, the monks from the abbey charitably supplied the two men with food.

Sadly, the two brothers fell victim to the dreaded plague then ravaging Paisley. The monks found them lying in the cave, locked in each other's arms in their agonising death throes. Out of pity, the ministering monks, mercifully buried them in the cave where they lay.

The burial mound where the two brothers lay was shunned as a place of evil repute and of danger, for centuries thereafter. When Gordon's Loan eventually became a thoroughfare, it was built in a curve to skirt round the mound. This unconsecrated mound where the Gordon brothers lay buried, ever after gave their name to the street. That was the legend.

However, the origin of one of the oldest street names in Paisley may be more mundane. The ground now forming part of the street was feued in 1404, by John de Lithgow, Abbot of Paisley, to Gilchrist Leche and his heirs. It was bounded to

A Victorian view, looking up Gordon's Loan leading to Causeyside. Prussia Street which was the shortest street in Paisley, leads off to the right and is now the site of the old fire station. The "Grecian bend" so beloved by the old weavers is clearly visible.

the rear by the Espedair Burn and to the front by the great orchard of the abbey. The ancient name given to this piece of ground was "Guna Chanys," which meant a crooked corner. It was aptly named, because the ground followed the crooked course of the Espedair Burn.

By 1490, an actual route existed between the Leche family property and the abbey orchard. This route connected to Causeyside at one end, skirted around the abbey orchard and led to the ancient mill at Seedhill at the other. In 1504, the lands of "Guna Chanys" were still occupied by the Leche family. Records of the time show that one of the family, Margaret Leche, married a Patrick Gordoun. Her husband most probably built more houses on their property fronting the street. As far back as 1573, the land they owned was being called Gordon's Loan.

In 1592, the then widowed Margaret Leche conveyed the property to her "well -beloved lawful son and heir, Patrick Gordoun".

Leitche's Land was built upon in 1700, when one-storey, thatched, weavers' cottages appeared. The curved street, Gordon's Loan, also became more built-up over the years. In 1744, houses began to be built on the other side of the road, where the ancient abbey orchard once stood.

Today Gordon Street, one of Paisley's oldest thoroughfares, is a busy one-way street. As you hurriedly drive pass the bend at the old fire-station, make sure your driving doesn't 'cave in' at the thought of the poor Gordon brothers fate!

High Church

In Paisley churches a miracle is a rare thing, but the High Church, built on a commanding site on top of Oakshaw Hill, was indeed a miracle. It was a miracle of design, thanks to an ingenious local architect, John Whyte. Under the large span of its new roof, 3000 Paisley worshippers could be seated. When the building was opened in 1754, a fellow architect stood, amazed and stated, "Though the area be so large, it has no pillars!" He added, "The construction of the roof is very curious and admired by men of taste."

The church was built to serve the needs of the burgh council, but the council's funding for the new building was meagre and most of the money was raised by subscription from wealthy Paisley merchants. The merchants who joined the congregation may have

The old High Church opened in 1754. The steeple was erected in 1776, both designed by Bailie John Whyte.

assumed that this gave them the right to have a say in the new church affairs. But, early in the church's life, when the question of who really ran the church arose, the council or the congregation, the first minister soon found out. He discovered that the council had first call on the church's takings. He left the church!

In May, 1776, after three years building, a handsome steeple was added to the church and a great bell was proudly set into position. The bell was rung until 1820. While being rung to celebrate the coronation of King George IV, the old bell finally cracked. It was replaced three years later by a heavier bell.

Locals named it "Roarin Tom" in honour of a Paisley gentleman, Thomas Farquarson, who had been the most active in getting up subscriptions for the new bell. When it was fixed in the steeple and rung for the first time, the people of Paisley thought "Roarin Tam" was the best bell in Scotland. But it did have a serious fault. It had a habit of throwing its clapper into Church Hill! On one occasion, it narrowly missed a group of church elders, gathered at the church door. One Paisley wag wrote,

When the old bell of 1866 finally cracked, a recast of this bell made by Duff & Sons, Greenock, was finally hung in 1872. It is this bell that still calls the congregation to worship each Sunday.

"The last rejoicing that ye rung,
Ye like a fool, flung oot yer tongue".

Like its predecessor, "Roarin Tam" cracked in 1865, while ringing out the death knell of Prime Minister Lord Palmerston. It was replaced in 1866. During this time, the High Church and Paisley Abbey both claimed their bells gave out 'messages'.

The minister of the High Church claimed that his bell said "We're a' gaun tae Heaven". Not to be outdone, Paisley Abbey's minister replied, saying that his bell said "I doot it!".

Quasimodo, would have had a difficult time in Paisley, ringing "The bells, the bells", of the High Church, which were always cracking and losing their tongues. This was bad news for the bellringer, but even worse, in 1833, the question of who had the right to ring the bells, the church or the council, was hotly debated.

That year, the town council was elected for the first time by ratepayers and councillors lost many of their old privileges. No longer could they parade on Sundays to the High Church, preceded by the Town's Halberdiers and no longer could they hold reserved seats in what they considered to be the town's church. With this loss of dignity, members of the council decided to hang on to what little power, if any, they had over the High Church.

Symbol of the heart
embedded in the pavement.

The councillors insisted that they had the right to ring the High Church bell for calling meetings of any kind, both sacred and secular. The political meetings they held in the church caused great offence to the congregation.

Soon a war of petitions and pamphlets was being fought between church and council about who could ring the bell. Eventually, after much litigation, the church won. The House of Lords had declared, "A bell is used in burghs for calling their courts and meetings, but we would like to know by what authority they call this bell of the High Church, a town's bell? It is not even supplied by the town, but by private subscription of the inhabitants".

Behind the present day church, now called Oakshaw Trinity, symbols of a handkerchief, a heart and a pair of glasses are embedded in the whinstone pavement. Legend has it that this marks the spot where a mason, working on the spire, accidently fell.

However, a more unlikely explanation was given in 1825, when a local newspaper, the "Paisley Advertiser", published a spurious article. The newspaper claimed that a mysterious, fairy-like figure called "Wee Leach" could be seen perched on the top of the High Church spire smoking his pipe. It was reported that large crowds of curious onlookers had gathered on Churchill Brae to get a glimpse of this little wonder. From all parts of the town, weavers abandoned shuttle and loom and came to see for themselves. Those blessed with good eyesight swore they saw him, others deficient in sight did not, but soon acquired glasses of all shapes and sizes to try and see the little wonder. This may account for the glasses in the pavment!

Next time you pass the old High Church, beware of the thunderbolt clapper falling from the skies and don't forget your glasses...you might catch a glimpse of Wee Leach!

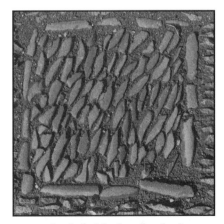

Symbol of the handkerchief
embedded in the pavement.

The Fall and Rise of John Mair

Cross Steeple and Tollbooth. Paisley's Town Hall and Gaol stood at the corner of Moss St / High St corner until 1870.

All had gone well in building the town's new tollbooth and steeple in 1757. The imposing spire rose 81 feet above the tollbooth roof. Each storey of the steeple rose up in elegant proportions, relieved by moulded cornices. Four clocks were surmounted with finely carved, stone vases at each corner. Above the louvred belfry rose the stone steeple, finished at the top with a ball finial and a gilded weather-cock.

Pride in the nearly completed new building suddenly turned to panic.

A local twenty year old mason, John Mair, had just fixed the weathercock to the top of the spire. When he was descending, he slipped on the scaffolding. As he fell, he managed to grab hold of a projecting stone.

Far below him, for the next fifteen minutes, people could be seen running with feather beds, some crying out for him to hold on, some standing with bated breath, women wringing their hands with anxiety.

When enough bedding had been gathered in the street, John dropped. He landed safely, to the great relief of the crowds, one of whom helped break his fall with his hands. John's life had been miraculously saved, but his leg was broken, leaving him lame. The only thing John had to say about his remarkable escape was, "By this fall, I shall rise".

And rise he did. He gave up the mason's mallet to become a weaver. In 1761, he became a manufacturer of muslins and lawns. To market his products he walked to London, despite his lameness, carrying a pack of his sample cloth patterns. On one occasion he called in at a fashionable London shop to demonstrate his wares, but an arrogant shop assistant ordered him to leave. John stood firm. The shop assistant, losing all patience, snatched John's Scotch bonnet, threw it outside and told him to follow. John picked up his bonnet, came back in and said with a wry smile, "Man you'll surely look at them noo?" The shop owner overheard the whole scene. He asked to see the contents of his pack and was so taken aback with the beauty and originality of the designs that large orders were placed.

The mansion house of Plantation Estate, Govan,
which was owned by John Mair until his death in 1824.

Soon he was to become an eminent merchant, operating as "John Mair, Son, Thomas and Co.", selling Scotch lawn and muslin from his warehouse at 60 Friday Street, London. He opened another similar warehouse in Glasgow.

At one period, however, his business suffered a severe loss. One of his ships was wrecked and it was uninsured. Due to his high moral character and business acumen, his creditors granted him an extension of time to repay his debt. They were not disappointed. Soon afterwards, he invited them all to his house and, sitting down to table, each found under his plate the money owed.

In 1793, such was his wealth, John Mair bought the 80 acre estate of Plantation in Govan and spent £30,000 on its improvement. In 1821, he acquired the stone which had saved his life as a young man and built an alcove on this estate to house it. He placed "the saving stone" on a pedestal, just like an altar. The undressed stone was treated as a precious relic. Despite all his wealth, he did not forget the man who had broken his fall with his hands. Discovering that he was poor, Mair gave him a pension for life.

To remind himself of his escape from death, he had emblazoned on the side of his carriage the motto "I rise by a fall". Above this was the figure of a swan to commemorate his mother's maiden name.

In 1785, he erected a monument to his parents in the Laigh Church yard, New Street, Paisley (now Paisley Arts Centre), which can still be seen. It reads;

In memory of his respected parents,
William Mair, late mason in Paisley, who died 23rd January 1763, aged 46;
And Marion Swan, his spouse who died, February, 1779, aged 72.
Erected by John Mair, Merchant, London.
Four of John Mair's children were also buried there.

John Mair died in 1824 and is buried in Govan Parish Church graveyard. At that time, rumour among the old Govan weavers said the "saving stone" covered his grave, but this was not so. One authority stated that the stone was removed from the garden of Plantation House some years after the old gentleman's death and rebuilt into the wall of another mansion house called "Craigiehall"in Bellahouston, where it was known as "The Mair remembrance stone". Another source tells us that the stone was eventually removed from Plantation House and given, in 1870, to John Mair's grandson , who at that time stayed in London.

John Mair lies in Govan, without his beloved stone to mark his grave. Perhaps his "stone of destiny" was destined to go elsewhere. John Mair's true memorial is not a stone, but his remarkable story of survival.

The tollbooth, the scene of John Mair's lucky escape, was demolished in 1870.

Some stones from the old building can still be seen in Brodie Park, beside the Dooslan Stane. A re-cast of the old tollbooth bell still hangs in the former Lylesland Church in Stock Street.

John Mair's splendid monument in memory of his parents.
This can still be seen in the Laigh Kirk yard in New Street.

Rev. John Witherspoon

Rev. Dr John Witherspoon
1723-94

In 1762, a great scandal occured in Paisley. The scandal was caused by rich, young men who were members of the Laigh Church congregation in Paisley's New Street.

Tradition has handed down that a number of young men from Paisley belonging to the aristocracy of the town held a 'mock communion' in a house in Church Hill. Ever since that time, it was claimed, the house has been haunted and the all the young men involved in this sacriligious act came to an untimely end.

But if the truth be known, it was said that the profane act of holding a 'mock communion' was held in a house in Orchard Street, on Saturday afternoon, 6th February 1762. Two Paisley manufacturers had invited two acquaintances to dinner. Soon they were joined by several others to take a glass of punch. As the evening wore on, the young men drank more and more and eventually ended up in the street. Their drunken behaviour was witnessed by two females. Soon tales of their misbehaviour became the talk of the town and, like a rolling snowball, tales of their misconduct became exaggerated. When the story reached the ears of their minister Mr Witherspoon, a very strict narrow-minded man, he assumed that the young blades of his congregation had committed the grossest profanity by holding a 'mock communion.'

Six of the young men thought to be involved in the proceedings were brought before the Laigh Kirk Session on 16th February. On the Sunday following, before the real truth or falsehood of the matter could be found, Mr Witherspoon preached to his applauding congregation the enormity of the sin that had taken place in their midst. Further enquiry by the session found the young men guilty of the flagrant charges and it was decided that they were to be publicly rebuked and excommunicated from the church, a very serious matter in these days. The case was to be taken further by reporting them to the Presbytery of Paisley, who would no doubt censure the young men even more.

The Laigh Kirk, New Street, where Witherspoon was minister between 1757-1768.

The young men heard the Laigh Kirk's verdict with utter astonishment and were amazed that they had been convicted of offences that they swore had not ocurred. They appealed to the Presbytery for a review of the sentence pronounced against them.

After hearing the evidence, the "Presbytery unanimously found the first charge as to the celebration of the Lord's supper not proven, to the second charge as to drunkeness, not proven." Further charges of swearing and mimicking ministers in the act of praying were also found not proven.

Mr Witherspoon became frantic at the decision of the Presbytery and threatened to brand the offenders with infamy and disgrace, by publishing the sermon which had recently been applauded by his own congregation. The sermon "Seasonal Advice to Young Persons" was duly published naming the persons involved in the "atrocious riot and profanity". Soon the "brazen young dogs" of his congregation sued Witherspoon for libel in the Court of Session and they won their case winning £292 in the process! Witherspoon clearly had no defence. It took him four years to pay off his debt. But he had lost face in Paisley and could no longer command the respect he once held. He decided to leave Paisley having received a calling from America. He demitted his ministry at Paisley and sailed with his wife, who hated the idea of emigration to USA, on the good ship 'Peggy' from Greenock on 18th May 1768. He had left to take up the appointment as President of Princeton College New Jersey.

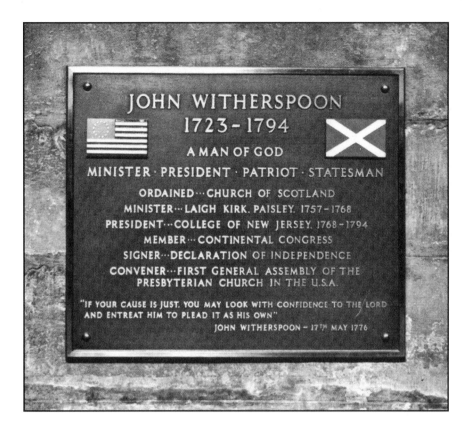

Memorial plaque to John Witherspoon. This can be seen in Paisley Abbey.

In America, Witherspoon re-organised and re-founded the college between 1768-1794. There, he taught many future leaders in American public life including President James Madison. Madison's Calvinist social and political thoughts reflected his teacher's great influence. Witherspoon entered politics as a Republican and became the representative of New Jersey to the Continental Congress during the years 1776-82. He helped to frame the American Declaration of Independence of 1776, of which he was a signatory. When King George III heard that America was no longer a colony of Great Britain, he blamed the entire loss on "That damned Presbyterian parson" Dr Witherspoon !

The young men accused of holding a mock communion, instead of descending into obscurity and poverty, in later life rose to positions of power and influence in the town. One of them was, in fact, to found the town of nearby Johnstone!

Paisley Pinks

A typical laced pink of the type bred in Paisley during the 18th & 19th Century which complemented the exquisite delicate designs then being produced on the town's looms.

The famous Paisley writer, Christopher North, spoke highly of the flowers which grew in the back gardens of his native town." What pinks! Aye we know them well, the beautiful garden plots...all round about our native town, pretty Paisley, and in among the very houses in nooks and corners that the sun does not scorn to visit."

In 1782, the weavers of Paisley established a Florist Society, the first in Scotland, which held exhibitions and competitions. This encouraged the culture of flowers of all colours and variety, but it was the improving of the pink which most interested them. One member, John Clark, is recorded in 1798 as "standing unrivalled in the culture of pinks...in various trials he generally came in victorious...different seedlings were raised by him of superior excellence". It was said of another member William Rose, "It is expected that no florist will in future vie with him". The pinks and carnations reared and exhibited in Paisley were highly acclaimed.

The raising of laced pinks in Paisley began in 1785, when some weavers sent to London for seed. Among the many plain seedlings grown, a few developed laced markings. From these, the ingenious Paisley weavers developed many new varieties which became known as "Paisley Pinks". Before long, they were supplying seed to England from their own stocks!

By 1800, Paisley growers had developed nearly eighty named varieties of pinks, while twenty years later, in the rivalry between London, Manchester and Paisley

A typical weaver's cottage, set in Lylesland, a rural area of Paisley.
In such well tended gardens, the weavers grew the famous Paisley Pinks.

growers, the local weavers could boast of over three hundred varieties. England could only manage one hundred! The "Kilbarchan Pink" was declared by Christopher North at this time as, "the loveliest flower on earth".

In 1806, John Finlayson sent some Paisley Pinks to Philadelphia. The recipient was his old friend Alexander Wilson, the exiled Paisley ornithologist. Wilson enthused about this gift, "I had the pleasure of receiving some of the finest pinks I ever saw, and which were greatly admired by our American florists here. I did not omit this opportunity of raising their admiration of the flora of my native country, by assuring them that these were but specimens of the inferior sort, and far surpassed by others of larger size and richer colours, which the gardens of a little village called the Seedhills of Paisley produces in the greatest luxuriance". These pinks may well have been "Finlayson's Bonnie Lass", bred in the Seedhills of Paisley by John Finlayson, who had been a member of the Paisley Florist Society since 1794.

Between the years 1810 and 1815, members of this society exhibited pinks between June and October. Competition to gain a prize was fierce.

In 1813, the prize of a silver snuff mill was awarded to Archibald Duncan for the twelve best pinks exhibited at the Paisley Florist Society. He was a gardener and seedsman at 100 Moss Street. James Finlayson of Seedhill won second prize.

The Society even won the sanction of the church. When the Paisley minister Dr. Ferrier gave the inaugural lecture of the Paisley Philosophical Institution in

1809, he referred to the Paisley weavers being known "not only for the execution of the most delicate ornamental muslins...but for the rearing of beautiful flowers". He remarked on the "peacefulness of their dispositions and the sobriety of their manners." The Society's elaborate programme of competitions and code of behaviour show it to have been quite strict and puritanical. This won the approval of the church of the day.

However, by the middle of the 19th Century, laced pinks had all but disappeared in Paisley. Specialisation in the cultivation of laced pinks had gone too far. The flowers became too stiff and formal and fell out of fashion. Also. with the advance of industry in the town, pollution and building expansion took their toll on the weavers' gardens. Finally, the weavers so cherished and guarded their pinks that it was difficult for outsiders to obtain original plants.

Paisley can be proud of her part in horticultural history although the famous "Paisley Pinks" are no longer with us. Perhaps the only reminder of past glories is the little laced pink called "The Paisley Gem", reputedly bred by John Macree in 1800, which still flourishes today in Paisley.

Although the Paisley Florist Society was founded in 1782, the first silver medal was only made in 1804 for the chairman of the society.

This beautifully engraved medal depicts the old Paisley Coat of Arms, under which appear a rose, a thistle and a shamrock.

(photo : courtesy Paisley Florist Society)

On the reverse of the chairman's silver medal appears a Paisley Pink springing forth from its pot.
(photo :courtesy Paisley Florist Society)

Poor Thomas Potts

Paisley from the East 1767. Centred in the picture is the old tollbooth at Paisley Cross, where Potts was hanged on the scaffold before a large crowd.
(picture:courtesy Paisley Museum)

For over two hundred years, the phrase "gone to pot", has become part of our every day language. The phrase has come to mean that something is ruined or destroyed, but how many people know that it originated in Paisley as "gone to Pott" and meant "gone to be hanged"? It was based on the tragic story of Thomas Potts, a weaver from Williamsburgh, who was hanged in Paisley in 1797.

One Sunday evening in March that year, four men, including Potts, broke into a farmhouse called "Gryffe Castle", in the parish of Houston. They were armed with bludgeons, large knives, cutlasses and swords. The ruffians brandished their weapons over the heads of the farmhouse occupants and threatened to kill the owner, Mr Barr. Shouting and swearing, the thieves demanded money. They

After Potts was cut down from the gallows, he was buried in an umarked grave
in the graveyard of the Laigh Church in New Street.

succeeded in stealing £12 in cash and carried away some valuable silver spoons.

Potts, a known thief with a previous conviction, was soon apprehended at his home, where the authorities found a large knife concealed in a barrel. One of the other robbers, Aitchison, was also apprehended. To save his own skin, Aitchison was to turn crown witness against his friend Potts during his subsequent trial. The other two thieves absconded and, despite a reward of £10 for their capture, were never found.

Potts was held prisoner in Paisley Tollbooth, where he complained that he was "ill-confined" in a small cell, where the jailor, Hart, kept a close eye on him.

In the 18th Century, theft was a serious crime, so Thomas Potts was sent for trial at the spring circuit court in Glasgow. Since he was also accused of attempted murder, the case was referred to the High Court in Edinburgh. Potts was tried there, on 12th July 1797. He pled not guilty, but the jury returned a verdict against him and he was accordingly condemned to death.

While he was a prisoner in the tollbooth in Edinburgh, he wrote a letter to his wife who had remained at home in Paisley. He told her of his tragic circumstances, "I am to be brought to Paisley on Monday, 7th, August, and to suffer on Thursday 17th day of the same month". Potts was brought to Paisley in the company of thirty-one mounted guards, who safely conveyed him to the condemned cell of Paisley Tollbooth. Here, he was visited by all the clergymen of Paisley and he chose to be accompanied to the scaffold by the the Rev. William Ferrier of Oakshaw Associate Congregation.

The place of execution was to be at the corner of the tollbooth, where a projecting beam or gallows stretched out from the steeple, so that the crowds in the High Street and Moss Street and at the Cross could witness the execution.

Mr Patison, who was the town's master of works, was in charge of the construction of the gallows. As he stood on the platform examining the quality of the workmanship, he looked down to the crowd that had gathered to view the awful apparatus. When he observed a local worthy, daft Rab Hamilton, he asked him to come up and try how the scaffold would fit him. Rab quickly replied, "Try it thysel, for thou's as cunning as me, and kens how to work it"!

The day of execution arrived. In front of a large, excited crowd, the condemned man emerged from the tollbooth, accompanied by the minister. He was placed on the platform or 'drop" with a hemp rope around his neck. Then, "a cruel pause occurred" when the bolt holding up the platform jammed. The hangman tried frantically to release it, but failed. This embarrassing delay caused concern to all who witnessed the scene. One of the town's tradesmen, either out of mercy for the wretched Potts, or from the fact that he may have been responsible for the fault in the apparatus, came forward. He lifted his foot and gave the bolt a smart kick. As he did so, he exclaimed to the hangman, "You doitit (stupid) devil!" Potts was, mercifully, despatched instantly. His body hung on the gibbet for a full hour and was finally cut down at 4-30 pm.

That evening, the magistrates of Paisley entertained themselves to dinner in the Saracen's Head Inn and drank rum, whisky, porter and beer, to end what had been an exciting day. Even the hangman and his assistant were given cordial hospitality at the inn, by way of thanks for their gruesome help.

James Maxwell, the self-styled "Poet of Paisley", published a pamphlet recording the whole proceedings. It was aptly named "Observations on the awful execution of Thomas Potts". He also wrote a verse for the occasion.

"Four out of four, but one is yet convicted,

On whom just punishment can be inflicted,

For two are fled, and one traitor turned,

To get his just reward a while adjourned".

After Potts was cut down from the gallows, he was buried in an unmarked grave in the graveyard of the Laigh Church in New Street. Paisley was glad to see the end of the whole messy affair, as many in the town had some sympathy for the hapless Thomas Potts.

R.A. Smith

R.A. Smith.(1780-1829)

Robert Tannahill, Paisley's weaver poet, is famous for his poems and songs.

However, the success of some of his well-known songs was due in no small measure to his intimacy and association with his songwriter friend, Robert Archibald Smith. Each contributed to the celebrity of the other. The poetry of Tannahill and the music of Smith were so completely blended, that they were like "two cherries on the one stalk".

In 1800, the twenty-year old Smith came to Paisley from England and, through time, became acquainted with Robert Tannahill. The poet wrote of Smith,

"There is Rab frae the South, wi his fiddle and his flute,

I could list to his sangs, till the starns (stars) fa' out".

During his stay in Paisley, Smith and Tannahill formed a partnership unique in the annals of Scottish music and song. Here, Smith composed original music for the poet's songs, the most famous being "Jessie, the Flower o' Dunblane". This one song brought fame to the two men. When it was first published in 1808, one music critic likened the composition to a piece by Mozart.

Smith, like Mozart, had been a musical child prodigy. At an early age, he had taught himself to play the whistle, flute and the violin. He was adept at musical notation, had an acute ear and was an excellent singer. As a vocalist, "he was highly finished", his voice "was a light mellow tenor, his enunciation distinct and accurate".

He made his musical debut in Paisley, singing at a concert. According to all reports, he "sang in a style so exquisitely sweet, that his audience were charmed".

In 1803, Smith found another outlet for his burgeoning musical talents. He joined the Paisley Volunteer Military Band. Soon, the band was marching to his spirited marches and military quicksteps.

Sacred Music,

Consisting of the

TUNES, SANCTUSSES, DOXOLOGIES,

Thanksgivings, &c

Sung in

St George's Church, Edinburgh.

EDITED BY

R. A. SMITH.

Frontispiece of "Sacred Music", published in Edinburgh, 1825,
for the congregation of St George's Church, where Smith was precentor.

He became a music teacher and abandoned his trade as a hand-loom weaver, an occupation he hated. In Paisley, he composed his first song "O, Bonnie was yon Rose Brier", which met with great success.

Smith was an admirer of Robert Burns and, in the company of Tannahill and others, he attended the first meeting of 'The Burns Anniversary Society', held in Paisley in 1805. This historic meeting was the beginning of the world's first Burns Club. In later years, he was to become its President.

Smith's musical talent was called upon by Paisley Abbey, when he was appointed, in 1807, precentor of this noble church. The gifted musician brought innovations in church worship. The choir in the Abbey was called the "band". Smith re-shaped and improved it and, soon under his influence, the band reached

A lilting little doxology called 'St Mirren's' with words and music by R.A.Smith.
Written while he was precentor and bandmaster at Paisley Abbey.

a high pitch of excellence. It became famous throughout Scotland, for its "soft singing". As leader of this fine choir, Smith became a national figure. In 1810, encouraged by his success, he published "Devotional Music". This music was a model of simple grandeur and deep devotion.

Smith appeared at the Glasgow Musical Festival in 1821, where he distinguished himself as a perfomer on the viola.

In 1819, he published "Anthems", acclaimed as a splendid work and esteemed by every lover of sacred harmony. His greatest undertaking, however, was not in church music, but in the gathering together of some 600 old Scottish melodies. These ranged from Jacobite songs to works by Robert Tannahill.

They were published as "The Scottish Minstrel" and were completed in 1824. One year later, he completed "The Irish Minstrel". Smith was a prodigious worker. He left Paisley in 1823, to take up an appointment in Edinburgh as precentor of St. George's Church. Their kirk session appointed Smith to "improve the psalmody of the congregation" and regarded him as "eminently distinguished as a musician, composer and teacher of sacred music". A marked improvement in musical standards immediately took place.

Between teaching, editing musical collections and appearing at concerts in the capital, Smith flourished. He even found time to sing at York Musical Festival in 1825. That year, he published "Sacred Music". One monumental tune in this book, written by Smith for his congregation, was called "St George's Edinburgh". It is still sung in churches today with the words "Ye gates lift up your heads on high, ye doors that last for aye", and is a masterpiece of church music.

Smith continued to produce such 'wondrous works', until his untimely death in 1829. His death caused a deep sensation of loss both in Edinburgh and in Paisley.

In any history of Scottish song or Scottish psalmody, Smith's name must be mentioned with profound respect. He is remembered in Paisley with a plaque in Paisley Abbey and his portrait hangs In Tannahill's cottage, Queen Street. His best epitaph, however, is his church music and the delightful melodies he composed to accompany the songs of his friend Robert Tannahill.

When Smith was appointed, in 1807, as precentor of Paisley Abbey
this was the state of the majestic old building.

Paisley's Military Goose

The old tollbooth Jail at Paisley Cross with the adjoining Saracen's Head Inn, the favourite stance of Paisley's famous goose.

The most famous military character to endear itself to the people of Paisley was not a great general, nor an admiral, nor even a common soldier, but was, in fact, a lowly goose. In the early 19th Century, Paisley folks came to love this venerable bird as it strutted the streets around Paisley Cross, with all the command of a soldier on parade.

The goose's first arrival in Paisley was, to say the least, traumatic. The poor bird had come floating down the Cart when it was in heavy spate in the winter of 1800. It had floundered in the rush of water and become stranded at the foot of Dyer's Wynd. The goose was seized by a town official and eventually handed over to John Orr, landlord of the Saracen's Head Inn at Paisley Cross. There, the poor, distressed goose was confined in the stable yard and destined for the pot.

But its age saved it from being eaten. The cook in the inn, a tender hearted man, declared it to be "too old by half a century" and that "nothing but an ostrich's stomach could digest its iron frame". After a second opinion was given as to the goose's inedibility, the bird was dismissed and allowed the full, uncontrolled run of the stable yard at the inn. For nineteen years, the goose lived

The military goose on parade!

there in relative obscurity and was handed over to each successive landlord as part and parcel of the premises. But the goose's life of fame was soon to begin.

In the eventful years of 1819 and 1820, radical riots pervaded every quarter of the town. When government soldiers were brought in to quell the riots, the goose gave its first indication of an attachment to military life. The sight of a red coat and musket were attractions it could not resist. The roll of drum or bugle call found a willing listener in this feathered recruit.

Every day for many months, the goose was seen parading, slow and stately with measured waddle, in front of the town's tollbooth jail. It followed closely on the heels of the soldier guarding the jail. The goose stopped when he stopped and paced when he paced. It became a comical sight at the Cross of Paisley.

Night and day, this 'military' goose could be found at its adopted post outside the jail. When it slept, none could tell. Often a soldier could be seen sharing his rations with his new brother-in-arms. The goose continued in the faithful discharge of its duties, so long as a red coat marched and a musket gleamed in front of the tollbooth jail.

The goose became a figure revered in Paisley as if it was the principal goose who had saved Rome! At length, the goose forsook its station at the jail when the guards no longer paraded there. A new jail had been built in nearby County Place in 1821, making the old tollbooth jail obsolete.

However, the goose speedily associated itself anew with recruiting sergeants. As each new recruiting party came to town, the goose was sure to follow. To a recruiting sergeant, the goose would act as orderly, uncannily keeping behind him

The military goose in full stride!

at the regulation distance of three paces and a stride. As soon as one sergeant left town, the old goose ingratiated itself with his successor.

When a handful of the town's young men gathered around the sergeant to take the king's shilling, the goose was ever found, in dignified silence, thrusting its neck between the sergeant's legs. In this position, it stood as if listening intently to tales of battles won in distant lands.

To all and sundry hurrying through Paisley Cross, it would bid good morning with a most affectionate gabble. To horse and foot, to regular and volunteer corps, it was kind and attentive. Whoever wore his majesty's uniform was sure to be graciously recognised by this unique bird. Any military officer who chanced to walk near the Cross would find the goose dogging him as diligently as his own shadow.

Sadly by 1827, it was evident to all eyes that Paisley's feathered eccentric was sinking fast with old age. The goose had become almost blind and very lame. Its drumstick legs were barely supported by its webbed feet, parts of which had been broken off by its years of campaigning in the hard, cobbled streets. The lustre of its once snowy plumage had irretrievably gone. Yet, to the last, it hirpled over its old haunts to visit old friends.

The goose died that same year in its first Paisley home, the stable yard of the Saracen's Head Inn. At the time of its death, local folklore said that it must have been within a few years of reaching a hundred! The military goose was fondly remembered in Paisley. Many soldiers spread the tale of the goose who helped them guard the jail during the dreary night watches and accompanied them on their marches through the town. It was truly "a remarkable bird".

Hogg meets Tannahill

Robert Tannahill,
Paisley's weaver poet.
(1774-1810)

Two men met for the first time in Paisley, James Hogg and Robert Tannahill. To some degree, this meeting between the two famous poets could be compared to the meeting between Stanely and Dr Livingstone. There are two versions of the meeting, the first account by James Hogg himself.

In the spring of 1810, James Hogg, who was celebrated in Edinburgh literary circles as the "Ettrick Shepherd", had made the long journey from Edinburgh to seek out and find Robert Tannahill somewhere in the streets of Paisley. Hogg's mission was to find the man whom he held in high admiration as a fellow poet.

Hogg recalled his visit... "I once travelled all the way from Edinburgh to Paisley solely to see him. I supposed that when I arrived in Paisley, I had only to ask for Tannahill, the poet, but to my astonishment few knew who he was. I was sent from one Tannahill to another, and many others, but none of them the object of my search."

At last, Hogg found Robert Tannahill working at the loom in his cottage in Queen Street. Hogg recalled his first impressions of seeing and meeting the famous poet of Paisley. "He was a swarthy man, bearing no external indication of the intellectual lava tide that slumbered in his soul".

When he first met Tannahill, Hogg used his famous pen name, the "Ettrick Shepherd", by way of introduction. Tannahill looked at Hogg in absolute awe! When he was told told just how far his visitor had come "to look upon him", he was flattered and delighted. Hogg was invited to stay the night as Tannahill's most welcome guest. Hogg sat beside Tannahill all night long, as the Paisley man sang many of his best melodies. The two men from humble circumstances, one a weaver, the other a shepherd, shared their gifts of poetry and song with like minds.

The following morning, Hogg was obliged to start by coach from Glasgow on his return to Edinburgh. Tannahill accompanied the "Shepherd" on foot, as far as Crookston Road in Glasgow. When the coach was about to depart, Tannahill grasped Hogg's hand heartily and burst into tears. Hogg said to his new friend, "Robert, dinna' tak' things so serious, we shall often meet again, and, if you'll no

James Hogg the "Ettrick Shepherd"
poet and novelist.1770-1835

come to Edinburgh to visit me, I'll come back to Paisley to visit you". "No Hogg." Tannahill replied, "This has been the proudest day of my life, but it cannot be....." at this point, sobs choked his words. Hogg was astonished when, two months later, he read in the Edinburgh newspapers an account of the suicide of his new friend Robert Tannahill.

The second account is told by James Barr, Tannahill's friend and songwriter. Between 18th- 25th March 1810, Barr came from Glasgow to visit the poet in his Queen Street cottage. Barr writes that, when he was leaving the cottage the following morning, Tannahill saw him to the end of the street.

As the two parted, Tannahill looked to Sandholes in the distance. He saw two other friends, R.A. Smith and W. Stuart, in the company of three strangers. Tannahill told Barr to wait, saying, "There is something in the wind." They watched as the five men entered a nearby public house. Tannahill and Barr were invited to join the company. When Tannahill was introduced to the three strangers, it turned out that one was the famous poet, James Hogg. Hogg had just finished a tour of the Highlands and, being near Paisley, had expressed a wish to meet the weaver poet, Tannahill. In contacting Tannahill's Paisley friends, Smith and Stuart, Hogg had finally managed to track down the poet.

The whole party left the West End of Paisley and adjourned to the Sun Tavern in the town's High Street. There, Hogg was "enraptured in their company". It was a treat to see the instant friendship of the two bards. Physically, the contrast was striking, Hogg, healthy and confident, Tannahill, delicate, quiet and unassuming, but their minds were as one.

Hogg and Barr then made their way back to Glasgow and stopped at the staging-post called Three Mile House (now Half -Way House). They took a lift in a coal cart to Broomielaw Bridge, made their way by foot to the Glasgow Tontine in the Saltmarket and then parted.

Although they may differ slightly, what really matters in both stories is the fact that James Hogg, one of Scotland's most famous poets, admired Robert Tannahill and his works so much that he went out of his way to come and meet him.

Tannahill firmly grasps the hand of his departing friend, James Hogg,
as they say goodbye for the first and last time.

Tannahill regarded Hogg's visit as the greatest compliment of his life and it came at a time when he most needed it. In a letter written on April 1st to his special friend, James King, Tannahill stated that Hogg and himself "had a good deal of conversation about the poets of the day". However, despite the recent, stimulating meeting, Tannahill's depression became overwhelming. The troubled life of Paisley's poet ended on 17th May 1810 in the cold waters of the Candren Burn.

Robt. Tannahill.

William Motherwell

Portrait bust of Motherwell by James Fillans. This was the first commission given to Fillans, the local Paisley sculptor, by his friend Motherwell.

A man cannot help where he is born! This was true of William Motherwell who was born in Glasgow, but came to stay in Paisley at an early age. Here, he became one of the most distinguished poets, writers and antiquarians the town has ever produced. By every test other than birthplace, William Motherwell truly belongs to Paisley. The bicentenary of his birth on 13th October, 1797, was celebrated in Tannahill's cottage by members of Paisley Burns Club and the Tannahill Macdonald Club.

In 1812, Motherwell left Paisley Grammar School as Dux pupil, entered the legal profession and became a clerk in the Sheriff Clerk's office. There, he was observed by Sheriff Campbell, who noticed this day-dreamer of a boy sketching such romantic things as mediaeval armoured knights. Noting his skill, Sheriff Campbell gave him ancient legal documents to copy. When the work was completed, the Sheriff said, "I received facsimiles so perfect that it was difficult to tell the old from the new"! In later life Motherwell, a practical joker, was to use his remarkable skill to 'forge' poems of James McAlpie, one time Sheriff Substitute of Renfrewshire. Motherwell claimed that poems in McAlpie's handwriting had been found among old documents in Paisley Sheriff Court. So authentic and convincing were the poems, that one was sculpted on the Martyr's Monument at Woodside and ascribed to James McAlpie!

The young lawyer became Sheriff Clerk Depute in 1819. In Paisley, at this time, the 'Radical War' was in full swing. One of Motherwell's distasteful duties as an officer of the law was to raid the houses of suspected radicals in the search for weapons. On calling at the house of John Parkhill, one of the radical leaders, the ransacking soldiers found no weapons. Motherwell asked Mrs Parkhill if she

RENFREWSHIRE
Characters and Scenery.

Paisley :

The cover of Motherwell's poem "Renfrewshire Characters and Scenery". Published in Paisley in 1824, it shows the old Paisley Burgh coat of arms. This book is now extremely rare.

had any pikes or guns hidden. She replied she had nothing, only a spear. Motherwell, taken aback, asked to see it and Mrs Parkhill replied that it was her maiden name! Satisfied and laughing, Motherwell left.

On another occasion, he was not so lucky. As he was passing over the bridge at Paisley Cross, he was knocked over and seized by an angry mob of radicals. He was hoisted onto the parapet by the infuriated mob, who intended to throw him into the River Cart. He was rescued in the nick of time.

Neither the political distractions of the time, nor his occupation could quench his real enthusiasm which was poetry. In 1818, he contributed some writings to a Greenock publication called the "Visitor". In 1819, he edited a book,"The Harp of Renfrewshire". In this work, Motherwell was the first to gather a collection of old and new songs and poems written by Renfrewshire bards.

Using the pen name, 'Malachi Malagrouther' Motherwell published pamphlets to defend the virtue of young Paisley women. A divinity student, John Birkmyre, had accused them of being 'loose' women for attending the newly-fashionable dancing assemblies in the town! Birkmyre wrote his scurrilous pamphlets under the assumed name of Bramble and had them distributed to each family who had patronised the dancing assemblies. Motherwell, like one of his favourite knights in shining armour, first "washed his spear" in this battle of words, rescued the ladies in question and became their champion. This episode showed Motherwell's ability with words which made him conspicuous as a writer, author and journalist in later years.

His literary career now flourished. In 1824, under the nom-de-plume Isaac Brown, he published "Renfrewshire Characters and Scenery". In one verse of this poem he extolls the virtue of a Paisley drink called "Pap-in". This was simply a glass of whisky papped into a beer.

"Pap-in! thou beverage of the gods-Pap-in!

That gives a soul to him who may have none,

In every club thou swellest every skin

Like Arab bottles. Whatsoe'er the sun

Can do for earth, by thee, for us is done.

Beneath thy sway life is both warm and bright;

Like Docks and Dandy-lions Wit and Fun,

Spread forth their beauties to thy genial light;

Wise saws, like haws and hips, thick clustering to the sight."

In 1827, his monumental work "Minstrelsy Ancient and Modern" brought him national fame as an antiquarian. During research for this work, he corresponded with Sir Walter Scott.

In 1828, Motherwell, with several Paisley gentlemen, established the "Paisley Magazine". It was never dreamt that such a high class work could be produced in a provincial town like Paisley. Motherwell had his doubts about the literacy of possible readers in Port Glasgow! He wrote.

"When mune and stars dance on yon hill,

And grass grows ower the tallest tree,

When cockle shells turn siller bells,

Port-Glasgow -Taste may dwell in thee".

William Kennedy, a close friend of Motherwell, retired as editor of the "Paisley Advertiser" newspaper and recommended Motherwell for the post. At his retiral dinner in 1828, Kennedy described his replacement as "honest as the steel of Damascus, a perfect journalist, a genius of first rate power" who would double the circulation in no time!

Motherwell later became editor of the "Glasgow Courier" and contributed to another Glasgow newspaper called "The Day". Many amusing articles such as "Memoirs of a Paisley Baillie" appeared from Motherwell's pen. In 1832, he published his best poems "Narrative and Critical", dedicated to his friend Kennedy. One poem "Jeanie Morrison" appeared here. He had first written it as a schoolboy, in secret admiration of an attractive blonde classmate and the poem still stands as one of his best works.

In collaboration with James Hogg, "The Ettrick Shepherd", he edited an 1835 edition of Burns, contributing a major part of the poet's biography.

Possibly through his friendship with the Irishman, William Kennedy, Motherwell became the district secretary of the Orange Society. He was called to London to give evidence to a House of Commons Committee when the society

The ladies who attended the fashionable dancing assemblies in Paisley were accused by John Birkmyre, a divinity student, of being 'loose' women. Motherwell, through his writing, defended their honour.

was under suspicion for its activities. The proceedings in London were held with a view to its suppression. Motherwell collapsed while giving evidence. On his return, he appeared to have recovered, but on 1st November, 1835, he died of a stroke in Glasgow.

William Motherwell left behind a treasure trove of literature and Paisley is proud of him. His birthday was honoured in Tannahill's cottage on his bi-centenary and his memory toasted with a "Paisley Pap-in". We can be sure that his miniature portrait bust, which hangs above the fireplace in the cottage, looked down upon us mortals and said,

"All earth below, all heaven above,

In this calm hour, are filled with love".

W. Motherwell

Seventeen years after Motherwell's death a monument in the form of a small Gothic temple was erected over his remains in the Glasgow Necropolis. Part of the monument shows the schoolboy William Motherwell in raptured gaze with his childhood sweetheart Jeanie Morrison, who became the subject of one of his earliest and best known poems.

This view of Paisley of 1826 was familiar to William Motherwell. The old Abbey Bridge gracefully spans the River Cart, just below the Hammills. The remnants of the abbey appear on the right. The steeple in the centre is the town's tollbooth and to the left rises the High Church steeple. Motherwell described the scene "Oh, 'tis a sight worth ten miles walk to see".

Paisley's Twelve Just Men

St George's Church, where a celebrated trial for high treason took place in 1830.

At the junction of George Street and Wardrop Street stands the old St George's Church, a building now converted to flats. It was completed in 1820 by the town council, to replace the Laigh Kirk in New Street which had become too small for Paisley's ever-growing number of worshippers. The new church was to be called St George's Low.

William Reid, the architect, designed the new building in the classical manner. Its main facade, fronted by four large Ionic pilasters, supported a pediment with quadrant shoulders. The church interior was well-appointed and could seat 1200 people. An octagonal steeple was planned to rise above the main facade, but was never built as the church treasurer absconded to South America with the money set aside for the building of the steeple! He was never brought to trial.

However, trials of a different order did take place in this church. These were trials for high treason!

In 1820, the goverment had some old scores to settle with the 'radicals' of Paisley. Most of the men wanted for their involvement in the radical riots of 1816-1819 left Paisley in a hurry and usually ended up in America. Those thought to be implicated and who had not fled were caught and imprisoned.

Mr James Coats, a member of the jury at the famous trial, who refused to condemn the two Paisley men of high treason.

Two such unlucky local men were James Speirs and John Lang. They were brought from Paisley Prison, manacled to two police officers, in a coach guarded by a troop of hussars. In the newly completed church building, they were put on trial, accused of high treason for which the penalty was death.

Leading judges from England and Scotland, picked government men, presided over the proceedings which were conducted according to English law. They were determined that the two men be hanged as an example to others.

Spiers was tried first. The government hoped to prove that, as the leader of a strike which closed down a local cotton mill, Speirs intended to subvert the constitution and plot against the king. The trial lasted a long three days.

The court insisted that the verdict of the jury must be unanimous. When only ten of the twelve-man jury returned a verdict of guilty on the capital charge of high treason, this was not acceptable to the court.

Mr James Coats (founder of the thread mills) was one of the two jurors who dissented. No efforts were spared by the rest of the jury to cajole and browbeat the two into changing their minds. After much argument, the jury agreed a verdict of guilty on a lesser charge. This, once again, did not suit the government judges, who wanted the men to hang. Once more, the proceedings were repeated with the same result. When the jury withdrew for a fourth time, they were given the 'comforting' message that they would have no refreshment until they unanimously agreed on the original charge of high treason!

When James Coats was told this, he calmly stretched himself on a bench and addressed his fellow jurors, "I will die here if necessary, but the blood of an innocent man will never be on my head". The other dissident juror was equally firm in his support.

When the jury finally returned to court to report that their verdict was unanimous, the judges were relieved. Then they heard that these stalwart Paisley men had given a verdict of NOT GUILTY!

The same verdict given for John Lang. The judge angrily declared, "Tell the jury we have no further use for them." and released the prisoners.

After the verdict of not guilty was given the judge angrily declared,
"Tell the jury we have no further use for them."

Paisley folks had expected the worst and thought that the trial would have gone against both Speirs and Lang. The highest legal minds in Britain had been thwarted by Paisley men in this celebrated trial, which was reported in all the national newspapers.

On the release of Speirs and Lang, almost the whole population of Paisley burst out cheering and experienced "exulted joy at the fondly desired deliverance". As the defence lawyers came out of the court, they and the victorious defendants were carried shoulder-high through a large cheering crowd.

In the evening, a social gathering was held in the town to "celebrate the joyful happy escape of the prisoners rescued from the jaws of death and the blood-seeking prosecutors defeated". Who could put down Paisley men without a fight!

From the obituary written in the Paisley Independent Newspaper when James Spiers died in 1856, we learn the following...

"James Speirs was altogether an isolated, ill- informed, incompetent man to promote a rebellion. His energies were only those of a common workman. His means were limited, and his companions few in number. He was without wealth or influence to oppose the government of the day. Speirs, a poor tradesman, was the last man to be branded a rebel. He, like other workmen of his day were beyond all doubt, deficient in all the munitions of a rebel war. To subject such a man as Speirs to a trial of treasonable conduct, and, if possible to deprive him of his life months after his supposed crime was committed, was indeed a work of treachery." James Speirs died peacably, yet in abject poverty at 11 Old Sneddon Street on the 4th October 1856, having survived the legal attempt on his life by 36 years.

The Provost meets the King

King George IV.

When James Carlile, Provost of Paisley, received an invitation to meet King George IV at Holyrood Palace, it threw him and the town council into a state of frenzied loyalty.

No Hanoverian King had ever before visited the ancient Kingdom of Scotland. Sir Walter Scott had stage-managed all the details of the visit, which was to take place in the month of August, 1822. A "Tartan army", of 300,000 Scots was to converge on Edinburgh to "look upon the king", in many cases for the first time.

It was only proper that Provost Carlile and his Baillies should be invited to such a large "gathering of the clans", as they represented the third largest town in Scotland and an important one at that. At least, Paisley thought so.

Preparations for the visit to Edinburgh caused a flurry of activity in Paisley. In order to appear well-dressed for this auspicious occasion, entire new outfits were purchased from the local cloth merchant William Stirling, whose premises were situated in Paisley High Street. No expense was to be spared! Unlike most other civic authorities who bedecked themselves in tartan, the douce burghers of Paisley opted for outfits reminiscent of red-coated Hanoverian soldiers, perhaps hoping to catch the eye of the King! The order the town placed with William Stirling was as follows:

3 scarlet cloth coats with blue cuffs and collars, gilt buttons and silver lace loops on the collars.

One scarlet cloth jacket with all the above.

One scarlet cloth coachman's coat with all the above.

5 blue cloth vests with gilt buttons.

5 pair blue plush small clothes.(breeches)

3 pair silk stockings.

1 pair white cotton stockings.

5 pairs of gloves.

5 cocked hats with a silver loop to only one.

James Carlile, Provost of Paisley
from 1822-1824.

The cost of all this amounted to a whacking £35-00, a considerable sum in these days. It was noted that due to the expense, the uniforms were to be saved for use in the future. Typical Paisley!

The next item on the expenses list was the purchase of a suitably engraved service of plate, to be presented to a Miss Montgomerie, in whose house they were to lodge overnight in Edinburgh. This little token of thanks was to set back the council £24-00!

To ensure the Loyal Provost and his entourage got safely down the Royal Mile to be presented to the King at Holyrood and back to their quarters in Queen Street, Messrs. Thomas and Mackintosh, Glasgow coachbuilders, were entrusted with repair and restoration work on an old Landau coach. Again, no expense was spared! The seats were re-upholstered with scarlet cloth laced with a blue fringe, specially dyed for this Royal affair. The carriage steps were covered in a plush, red leather. A float with silver lacing adorned the carriage. The window frames were fitted with new black velvet. The body of the carriage was painted in yellow and black and finished in varnish. No red, white and blue for the men of Paisley! As a matter of civic pride, each carriage door was emblazoned with the Paisley coat-of-arms. This item alone cost two guineas! The total bill for works on the carriage amounted to £22-00!

When the great day came, the Provost and Baillies of Paisley left their elegant apartments in Edinburgh's Queen Street in their splendid open-top carriage. Two town officers, in scarlet coats and cocked hats, mounted in front and two footmen in the back, similarly dressed carrying white staves, made a grand appearance. As they passed through the crowds down the Royal Mile a few spectators from Paisley, justly proud of them, cheered as they passed.

Once into the Palace, one of the Paisley Baillies mistook the Lord Mayor of London, Sir William Curtis, for the King and proceeded to do homage to him. Sir William was dressed in full Highland costume and had a grand personal appearance, such as the Baillie expected to find in His Majesty.

A court official hastily laid hold of the bewildered Baillie and led him forward in the proper direction, where he was graciously smiled upon by His Majesty,

either because of his loyalty, or more probably for his attempted performance before Sir William.

This loss of dignity before His Majesty was bad enough, but more was to follow. On leaving the Palace, our civic representatives, who were in full court dress and wearing cocked hats, found their carriage and the two town officers were missing!

The two in question had sneaked off to a hostelry in the Canongate for refreshments, not thinking for a moment that it was possible His Majesty had parted so soon with their worthy Provost and the Baillies of the ancient Burgh of Paisley!

So the loyal lieges of Paisley, in a most undignified fashion,

After leaving the palace, the Provost and his Baillies were astonished to find their carriage missing. Their two drivers had nipped in for a quick one in the Canongate!

had to walk to the Canongate in pursuit of their carriage and officers, to the considerable amusement of the crowds. After some time and with some difficulty, they found their runaways. They, not in the best of humour, were then conveyed back to their rooms in Queen Street. We can only imagine the angry scenes that followed.

The total cost of this council junket amounted to a staggering £164-00! The magistrates personal expenses, alone, amounted to £54-00, a year's wages for a competent Paisley weaver.

In contrast to this, four young, thrifty Paisley men made their own way to Edinburgh to see King George 1V. They stayed for an enjoyable week with full board and lodgings and the cost amounted to only £1-00 each. When they returned to Paisley, they heard scandalous rumours about the total cost of the Council trip to Edinburgh. They were of the opinion that, "when reckless and ostentatious expenditure is the order of the day, enjoyment and comfort can not be guaranteed". Sometimes it can prove, to say the least, a total embarassment!

The original invoice from William Stirling, cloth merchant,
for rigging out the council junket to Edinburgh.

The original invoice for purchase of a service of plate, presented to Miss Montgomerie,
the landlady in whose house the party stayed overnight in Edinburgh.

William Lyon

Paisley Cross in 1835, where the arrival and departure of stagecoaches between Paisley, Edinburgh, Glasgow and London caused great excitement.

Paisley Cross is always a scene of bustle and activity. It was no less so in 1822, when the arrival and departure of the stage coaches which ran between Paisley and Glasgow caused great excitement. At this time, there were at least five companies running coaches from Paisley, making a total of eighteen arrivals and departures each day. Competition between the coaches companies was fierce. However, the most popular as far as Paisley was concerned was the coach service run by William Lyon.

Lyon was a native of Paisley and, as a youth, apprenticed to the loom. Disliking the dull life of the weaving trade, he joined the army and enlisted in a regiment of artillery. He saw his first major action in 1807 during the Napoleonic Wars. He took part in the bombardment of Copenhagen, when the British destroyed the Danish fleet lest it fall into Napoleon's hands. After this, he served in the Peninsular War with Wellington. Later, in 1809, he played a brave part in the disastrous retreat to Corunna with Sir John Moore. Unlike his commander, Lyon survived and was promoted to the rank of sergeant-major for his good behaviour, discipline and bravery.

THE

Sons of Commerce,

AND

FAIR TRADER,

Coaches.

Messrs. LYON & FRASER

Most respectfully beg leave to announce to their friends **and** the public, that their Coaches will now run by **RENFREW**, at the following hours, viz.

From PAISLEY, at 10, half-past 10, 11, 12, 3, 5, and 7 o'clock.

From GLASGOW, at 12 noon, 3, half-past 3, 5, 6, 7, and half-past 8 evening.

Messrs. L. & F. trust these arrangements will meet with general approbation, the road being undoubtedly the pleasantest in the West of Scotland ; and, in consequence of its superiority, they will be able to run it in the same time as they did on the former one. Passengers not residing on the new line of road, and wishing to be taken up, the Coaches will call for them previous to coming to the Office :—they therefore hope that a descerning public will still continue that support, which they have so liberally given these Coaches.

Poster advertising Messrs Lyon and Fraser's
proposed new coach run to Renfrew in 1824.

In 1822, on leaving the army, he returned to Paisley and became a coach proprietor. He set up business in St. Mirren's Square (now George Place), where he had a coach-yard and stabling for his horses. Lyon called his coaches "The Sons of Commerce" and started running them between Paisley and Glasgow in June 1822. They quickly became popular, since fares were offered at greatly reduced prices, much to the chagrin of his competitors. Lyon also said that his customers need not give his drivers the customary tip. This was popular with the Paisley people!

With his amiable qualities and the attention he paid to his passengers' comforts, Lyon 's business grew and sent his competitors reeling. He and his first partner, Fraser, expanded the service to Renfrew in 1824, naming that coach the "Fair Trader".

To see one of the "Sons of Commerce" coaches arrive or depart at Paisley was a grand sight. Lyon's coaches were strongly built, yet had the appearance of being light and fast. They were beautifully painted in rich colours and were drawn by four proudly-apparelled horses in silver-plated, richly decorated harness. The coach driver was often Lyon himself, a handsome, tidily-dressed man with whip in one hand and the reins of the four-in-hand in the other. He had learned his driving skills during his days in the Horse Artillery. Lyon's improvements of cheaper fares and safe, reliable coaches made him known to his competitors as "The Celebrated Reformer of Abuses in the Stage-coaching Trade". Soon, he was to expand his business by running daily coaches to Johnstone, Renfrew, Kilmarnock, Saltcoats and Edinburgh. Coaches even went as far afield as London.

In 1826, the year of the "short corn", horse-feed rose to famine prices. Other local coaches gave up running that season, but Lyon managed to keep his coaches on the road, to the great relief of Paisley business men.

The following year, Lyon formed a partnerhip with a Mr Walker. Their coaches were now to run every half-hour. The proposed fares charged by this new partnership were... outside 9d, inside 1/6d and basket 1 shilling!

The partners advertised their new service to the public. "Messrs Lyon and Walker avail themselves of this opportunity of expressing their gratitude for the very liberal encouragements they have experienced from the public...and they beg to assure them, that their coaches will be kept on the road at moderate fares, a proof of which they have already shown by keeping running during the unprecedented high price of corn and hay last season... When other proprietors had taken their coaches off the road."

In his hey-day, William Lyon became so successful that, each day, two hundred passengers used his coaches between Paisley and Glasgow. Eventually, he had a monoply of the trade, but he never abused this position, always providing safe travel at a fair price.

The coming of the railways sounded the death knell of travel by stage coach. William Lyon lived to see the first "iron horse" arriving in Paisley in 1839. He died in Glasgow in 1848.

So respected was William Lyon in his native town, that it was stated, "If ever any gentleman was entitled to a public monument it was Mr Lyon."He will be remembered for his reform of abuses in the stage-coaching business in Scotland and England.

Cook's view of Paisley

James Cook's view of the abbey and surroundings in 1827.

Today, the town's ancient abbey stands in open surroundings for all to admire its splendour. But it was not always so. During the 18th Century a clutter of ramshackle houses, workshops and factories grew up around the building and, over the years, the view of the magnificent, mediaeval abbey was gradually blocked out. This was particularly the case in Abbey Close, where cheap, speculative, over-crowded housing, a large thread mill and some silk loom workshops had been erected. One lean-to house had even been built against the Great West Door of the abbey!

In 1769, a respectable working class church, belonging to the Burgher Congregation of Paisley, was built in Abbey Close. It was here that the young David Dale worshipped while he was an apprentice weaver in Paisley. Dale would later become famous as the founder of the New Lanark Mills.

The new church buildng was simple and unpretentious, but it was built directly opposite the West Front of the abbey and made viewing from a distance impossible. The Burgher Church's arrival in Abbey Close was one of the many results of 'asset stripping' of the old abbey and its surrounding gardens, carried out by James, Eighth Earl of Abercorn.

In 1827, the Burgher Church in Abbey Close was demolished. The plan was that a larger church would be built to house the growing congregation. However, when the site was vacant, the citizens of Paisley saw the wonderful vista which had been opened up. They could once again see the lofty west gable of their beloved abbey from Causeyside.

The feeling in the town was that the vacant site which now afforded such a magnificent view of the abbey should be kept as open space. With this in mind, Provost Boyd reported to the Town Council, "A very strong feeling appears to exist among the public that the view if possible, be preserved". The only snag was that, to achieve this, the congregation of the church would have to be offered suitable alternative sites.

The church initially agreed to the council proposals and work on their replacement church in Abbey Close temporarily came to a halt. The council offered three alternative locations, or £400 in cash, to entice the Burgher Church to move. A stipulation of the deal was that the church would enclose the vacated site with a stone parapet wall and iron railings to match the nearby part of the abbey. When the 'canny' church managers discovered that such conditions would incur a loss of £300, they refused to agree to the council's proposals. They decided in favour of building a bigger church on the same site, to seat its 800 worshippers.

Before the new church rose higher and higher to obscure the view of the abbey, one enterprising Paisley artist and portrait painter, James Cook, set up his easel at the foot of Causeyside to capture the scene. His painting not only captured the temporary open vista of the abbey, but portrayed a valuable record of people and the town scene in the Paisley of 1827.

The foot of Causeyside and St Mirren Street forms the foreground. The central figure is a man, wheeling a barrow filled with yarn, making his way up Causeyside. A carrier's van emerges from the bottom of St Mirren St with deliveries for the shawl warehouses of the Causeyside manufacturers (the 'Corks'). On the right is the portly form of John Hart in his knee breeches, wearing rig-and-fur white stockings. As the head jailor of Paisley Prison in County Square, he was a familiar figure in the town. While he was in charge of some prisoners during the 'Radical War' in Paisley, he heard them defiantly sing, 'Scots Wha Hae'. The king was not too popular in Radical Paisley! The prisoners soon heard John Hart rattling his keys at the cell door. Opening it he exclaimed, "Ye're a wheen O' deevils, I'll put ye in chains, an' shut ye up in darkness!" He carried out his threat! John Hart's other claim to fame was as a noted courser. He kept the best-trained greyhounds in the West of Scotland. His faithful racing dogs are seen at his side.

From 1827 until recent times, the rebuilt Abbey Close Church appearing on the right of the Town Hall obscured the view. Once again with the church's removal, the citizens of Paisley can almost enjoy the same view as portrayed by James Cook.

Near the bottom of St Mirren St, the artist faithfully portrayed the tavern called the Spirit Cellar. The tavern was owned by the local Saucel Brewery, famous for its 'A1 Scotch Whisky'. At the bottom corner, he shows bustling Betty Boyd, keeping her eye on her fruit and vegetables stall set up in the street. Her stall stands outside the Turf Tavern, a favourite rendevous of local traders and travellers who would nip in for a 'quick one' to seal the deal of the day.

To the right of the abbey is the Abbey Mill, with its steam-powered chimney stack reaching ever upwards. The buildings in the right foreground were shops and warehouses belonging to Messrs Gibb, Wright and Lochhead This was the starting point of Causeyside. Today, the street forms the bottom side of Dunn Square.

James Cook's painting became so popular with the 'Buddies' that, in 1836, it was lithographed, published and dedicated to the two ministers of Paisley Abbey, McLean and Brewster. James Cook, like his famous namesake, explored, recorded and charted a piece of Paisley for future generations of 'Buddies' to enjoy!

However, when the new church building was completed, the view shown in the painting was again obscured. The church, known as Abbey Close, stood until recent times. Now the only signs that a church once stood there are the old tombstones and, today, the abbey can again be seen from Causeyside.

Seestu!

SEESTU!

No. 1.   PAISLEY, TUESDAY, NOVEMBER 23, 1880.   Price One Penny.

'Seestu' was a weekly comic magazine first published in Paisley in 1880.
The price was one penny.(picture:courtesy Paisley Reference Library)

Ootlanders, that is persons not born in Paisley, have over the years questioned the origin of the word "Seestu". Compilers of most Scottish dictionaries have ignored it. Glasgow "keelies"poke fun at it, yet the mere mention of this word brings a smile to the face of the Paisley man.

"Seestu" is the nickname for the town of Paisley and has been so since around 1830. The name gives little clue as to its true origins.

Paisley, as everyone knows, has been the birthplace of poets and professors and has produced many men of "credit and renown". It has also produced a breed of men who, provincial in the extreme, "canny see past Paisley".

So it was, in 1830, that an English tourist visiting Edinburgh Castle, had for his guide a lank, keen-eyed, Paisley-born man, William Aitken. Aitken was exiled in Edinburgh, where he kept a tavern at the head of Leith Walk. The English visitor, keen to see the sights of Edinburgh with his appointed guide, became frustrated with the delay. The Paisley man had spent a long time extolling the virtues of his native town to this stranger. The visitor then said, "Now my good friend, you have talked quite enough about your native town, pray forget, Paisley

Professor John Wilson, better known as the writer Christopher North, was indeed the cleverest of them in 'Embro' College, and he was a Paisley man!

for a moment and let us look at Edinburgh."

Offended by this remark, the guide replied, "It's no easy to forget Paisley when you look at Edinburgh. Sees't you" , as he pointed, "That's Edinburgh University, where they come from England and a' pairts to learn to be doctors and members of parliament. It has the cleverest men in the kingdom for its professors, but the cleverest of them all is John Wilson, an he's a Paisley man.

Sees't you", pointing to a distant spire, "Yon's the steeple of North Leith. It's the best stipend in Scotland and, at this present time, it's got the best preacher in Scotland for its minister. You must have heard of the Reverend James Buchanan. You must have forgotten. He's a Paisley man. And, sees't you that kirk wi' the dome on it? That's St. George's Kirk, where all the gentry attend for the sake o' the singing and I'll warrant ye'll no hear the like o' their precentor in a' England. They ca' him R. A. Smith, and he's a Paisley man.

And, sees't you where a' thae coaches are waiting to start? That's the Register Office. Ye may say it's the keystane o' the kingdom, for Lairds and their lands a' hing by it. Although it's the place where Dukes and Earls keep their titles and the King himself keeps his papers, every day, when the clerks have gone home and the door is closed, the entire place is left in charge of an auld wife, and she's a Paisley woman."

Our worthy Paisley guide told a true story. The professor at the university was in fact John Wilson, famed as the writer "Christopher North". He was Professor of Moral Philosophy and mixed with the finest intellectuals of the day. To hold such a position, he was looked on as a genius. His statue still stands in Princes Street Gardens. A plaque marking his birthplace can be seen in Paisley High Street, opposite the library.

The precentor of St George's Kirk, Robert Archibald Smith, had been the precentor of Paisley Abbey, where he had become famous for his church music. While in Paisley, he also wrote several well-known lyrics for Tannahill songs. He then moved to Edinburgh, where he composed the rousing hymn tune, "St Georges, Edinburgh", still sung in churches today.

Over the years, Paisley Buddies adopted the name "Seestu" as a nickname for the town. It is mentioned time after time in local publications. There was even a weekly comic magazine called "Seestu", published between 1880-1. This only ran for twenty-three weeks and contained humourous articles and cartoons of local celebrities. It was printed from the offices of the Paisley Daily Express, then situated in Causeyside Street. Citizens of Paisley became known as "Seestuites".

There was even a Paisley-built motor car called a "Seetstu". Perhaps the variation in spelling indicated the car had an actual seat! It was a small, 3 horse-power, two-stroke engine built by James McGeoch & Company, at 11 Incle Street. Only six or seven were ever built. Perhaps the brand name was to blame!

The name of "Seestu", strange as it is, is enshrined in Paisley's history, all due to the wee Paisley man, who thought the world revolved around his home town. Believe it or not, this is a true story, but don't tell it in the streets of Glasgow!

Between the years 1894 -1911 these Paisley gentlemen held an annual holiday golf championship, the winner to receive the SEESTU medal. The winner of the coveted medal of 1910 is John Goudie seated centre.(photo courtesy:J.Goudie)

The Two Rabs

"But where's the calf? Ah'm ready for the calf noo!"

Rab Ha'

On market days in Paisley, the streets were once kept lively by ballad singers, street criers and hawkers, of a variety no longer to be seen today.

There were great numbers of simple-minded, eccentric people, who made a meagre living by selling matches or chap books. They mostly disappeared from the scene with the advent, firstly of poorhouses and asylums and secondly with the great improvement in our social and economic conditions, which we take for granted today. But it was not always so...

Take, for example, one famous character who, unlike most of us who eat to live, lived to eat! His name was Rab Ha'. Rab Ha' became famous as a glutton in Paisley, Glasgow and the West of Scotland in the early part of the 19th Century. It is thought most likely that he was born in Paisley, or at the very least in a part of Renfrewshire. One old Glasgow history book states that he had his headquarters in Paisley, although exactly where is not stated.

Rab had several nicknames such as 'Rough Rab' or 'The Renfrewshire Glutton'. In Paisley, he was known as 'The Paisley and Glasgow Glutton.' In Glasgow, a city which has claimed him as their very own, he is still fondly remembered as 'Rab Ha' the Glasgow Glutton'.

Occasionally Rab walked from Paisley to Glasgow and passed a certain farm.

Another well-known character in Paisley was Jamie Blue. He was a street singer, who at election times wrote poetry of sorts.

When the occupants saw him approaching, they would put on a large pot of porridge. This would be served up to Rab as he sat on the doorstep. Such was his appetite that he would sup the porridge from one of the bins usually used to feed the calves.

Before he took to 'eating for a living', Rab had been a farm servant. His real name was Robert Hall. In stature he was a large fellow, with a powerful build. His stomach had an unbounded capacity for food. Rab soon realised that by attending horse races, fox hunt meetings, town and country fairs or anywhere large crowds gathered, he could obtain free meals. If he was lucky, he could even earn himself some pocket money from the crowds.

Wealthy merchants and noblemen in Paisley and Glasgow made bets on Rab's enormous capacity for eating. One such wager was made by a Renfrewshire nobleman. He bet that Rab could eat a whole calf at one sitting! Rab was only too keen to eat the free meal and get money afterwards for doing so. What Rab did not know was that the three-month old calf was to be eaten in the form of pastries and pies.

The meal was duly prepared and served to Rab. In front of a large crowd, with the betting getting fiercer by the minute, Rab steadily munched and chewed through dozens of pastries and pies. Rab was in his element! As he reached over for the last pie, he paused. This action caused some consternation in the crowd, who were afraid that he could not complete the meal and so bets would be lost. But the bold Rab had only paused to drain a bottle of porter! The nobleman patron who had sponsored Rab and set him up, came up to him and asked, "Weel Rab, how are you getting on?" "Oh gay an' weel, my lord," replied Rab, "but where's the calf? Ah'm ready for the calf noo!"

'Rab Ha' died on November 1843. He was found dead in a hay loft in Thistle Street, Glasgow, and was buried in the Gorbals Cemetery.

Rab Hamilton

Paisley also produced another town character by the name of 'Rab'. Rab Hamilton was an inmate of the town's hospital or poorshouse. This was known locally as the 'Wee Steeple'. It stood in High Street until 1807, when it was demolished to make way for Orr Square.

The Wee Steeple, the town's hospital or poorhouse
where Rab Hamilton was an inmate.

In those days, Rab Hamilton, along with other inmates, was at liberty to go in and out of this building as though it was his own house. Although Rab was a wee bit simple in the mind, he was to be seen every good day walking about the town like a landed gentleman. He was often found where a new house was being built, resting himself in the masons' shed and talking to them.

He was in the habit of going about the town selling 'Parliament cakes", a type of gingerbread cake eaten by the members of the old Scots Parliament. He was perfectly willing to sell two cakes for a penny, but he would not sell one cake for one half-penny! If a penny was tendered, Rab was 'suspicious of his own ability' to give the correct change. Rab wandered as far as London, where, by accident, he met a fellow townsman, the wealthy Mr Fulton of Park, who was there on business. This gentleman shook Rab's hand and asked him, "What has brought thee here Rab?" "Na." said Rab, "What has brought THEE here?" The kindly Mr Fulton did not lose sight of this curious traveller, but found ways and means to send him home to Paisley.

Although Rab was a simple man, he also showed a great deal of shrewdness. In August, 1797, the robber Thomas Potts was to be hanged at Paisley Cross. The town's master of works, William Pattison, was to be responsible for the hanging, but was reluctant to perform the execution. Mr Pattison met Rab and told him in a very serious manner that he had a good job for him. "Aye," said Rab, "What is that?" "We are in great need of a hangman and, if thou likes to try thy hand, thou will be weel paid for it". "Dae it yersel!", said Rab, " Thou's as keen 'o siller as me."!

Cholera Riots

Cholera Morbus.

The best means of avoiding this Dreadful Disease are,

1. Fresh Air, as much as possible; only take care not to catch cold.
2. Be cleanly, in the House, and round about it; and in the Clothes and Skin. Open the Windows daily. *Clear out all Drains and Ditches* near you: and take away all heaps of Filth from near your House. Get it Lime-washed without delay.
3. Lead a regular and Sober life. Drunkards are among the first attacked and likeliest to die. Take Moderate Exercise.
4. Wear warm clothing, flannel next the skin, worsted or woollen stockings.
5. Be cautious and sparing in taking green vegetables, raw fruits, pork and salted meats. Let your diet be as simple and nutritious as possible.
6. Keep the feet always dry and warm.
7. Be cheerful and don't give way to a Dread of the Disease.

THE CHOLERA MORBUS BEGINS

Sometimes—with a common local complaint or purging. Neglect not this, or it may be fatal.
Generally—with Giddiness; Sickness or Vomiting; Shivering; Great Coldness and Blueness of the Skin; Extreme Weakness; Cramp, beginning in the Toes and Fingers, and so spreading all over the Body.

The first things to be done for those who are seized with it are these:

1. Put the Patient to Bed between *warm and dry* Blankets.
2. Send directly to the Doctor. Much depends on his speedy help.
3. Give to drink immediately two table spoonsful of common Kitchen Salt, dissolved in half a mutchkin of warm water for a grown person, and half that quantity for a child. This will produce vomiting.
4. Apply round the Arms and Legs bags of heated Bran, Ashes or Sand.—N. B. Worsted Stockings will do for bags. Rub the body briskly with a warm hand. Dry heat is better than moist.
5. Apply to the pit of the Stomach a poultice of equal parts of Flower of Mustard and Oatmeal, mixed together with boiling Vinegar.
6. In very bad cases, or if the Doctor should be long in coming, give from 30 to 40 drops of Laudanum in hot Brandy and Water with Peppermint; be sure to count the drops,—half that quantity will do for a child.
7. The Patient should not be allowed to sit up for the purpose of having evacuations. An upright posture is apt to bring on fainting, and sometimes death.

Keep this paper for your Direction, in case the Cholera should attack you.

THE CHOLERA MORBUS is a deadly plague, by means of which Almighty God has cut off great numbers of mankind. It kills often after a few hours' illness. It is our duty by all means in our power to preserve our own lives, and those of our Neighbours. For this end it is very needful to keep the Mind free from alarm. Now there is no way so sure of warding off the fear of death, as the answer of a good conscience towards God, and the hope of forgiveness and eternal life through Jesus Christ our Lord.

The Cholera cries aloud, " PREPARE TO MEET THY GOD !"

The handbill circulated in Paisley during the cholera epidemic in 1832. It informed the people how to avoid the dreadful disease, how to recognise the symptoms and what to do if you were seized with it. At the bottom, the ominous words appear "The cholera cries aloud, PREPARE TO MEET THY GOD!" (photo:courtesy Paisley Museum)

In the 19th Century, it was said of Paisley, "The town upon the whole, may be considered as a healthy place of residence, notwithstanding the occasional visits of epidemical disease". This unmentionable disease was the dreaded cholera. As the highly contagious disease was heading for Paisley and about to strike down

An old view of the slums of New Sneddon Street where the first case of cholera was reported. It was ironic that the town's hospital seen at the bottom of the picture was situated in this disease ridden area.(photo:courtesy Paisley Museum)

the citizens of the town, the Paisley Advertiser newspaper acted on instructions from the local health authorities and printed handbills. These were hurriedly circulated throughout the town. The handbills warned people of the dreaded symptoms to look out for and what precautions they should take "in case the cholera should attack you". The handbill ended with these words, "The cholera cries aloud, PREPARE TO MEET THY GOD!" Such a threat had not existed in Paisley since the last visitation of the Black Death in 1645.

Forewarned of its approach, the Town Council took business-like precautions against the spread of this dreadful disease. A temporary hospital was set up in Hutcheson's Charity School at Oakshaw. The 'fever dens', which were the overcrowded slum areas of the town, had their back-court middens and dungsteads speedily removed. Poor people were given free soap and their house walls washed down with lime. Small, overcrowded houses, particularly in the

Sneddon area, had their "ventilation secured". Ditches and burns and foul, slime-covered ponds were cleaned out. The local sanitary inspector later reported "Considering the nature of the water supplies, mainly from private wells, and the destitution existing in some parts of the town, it would have been nothing short of a miracle if Paisley had escaped the disease".

The first case, reported in February 1832, was predictably in New Sneddon Street, one of the slum areas. Significantly, the victim was a travelling hawker, Murdoch Galbreath, whom it was thought had brought the disease to the town. Within four days, nine people had died. From that time onwards, thirty new cases of cholera a week were reported.

Difficulties arose in getting the victims buried, as many were so poor that they had made no provision for burial. Due to the large number of deaths, a common graveyard was opened up at Paisley Moss, near the Racecourse.

At the height of the epidemic, the health authorities, such as they were, attempted to fumigate the streets of the town. Six large tubs filled with various chemicals were barrowed through the town. Citizens threw open their windows to allow the foul-smelling vapours to enter their houses. The belief of the times was that the dreaded contagion could be kept away by such means.

The town's medical men were rushing about to and fro, giving their services "unweariedly and and ungrudgingly." But the poorer, ignorant people in the town, who suffered most, viewed the doctors with great suspicion. When the doctors removed the dead bodies from houses, they were accused of being 'body snatchers', just like the infamous Burke and Hare from Edinburgh.

Riots began to take place as the numerous, shrunken, dessicated bodies were being removed for burial. Unruly crowds wielded pokers and knives and threatened to bury the doctors along with the victims of the epidemic. Shouts of, "Ye may be after taking him, but before ye's reach the Moss, every man and mither's son of ye's will be Burked, and chucked into the same hole!"

Meanwhile at the Moss burial ground, two shovels and a small piece of cord with an iron hook attached, were found abandoned. Some of the public thought this was clear proof that the "body snatchers' had been at at work during the previous night! When an angry mob went to the Moss, they found an empty coffin. This confirmed their suspicions. Rumours flew and town gossip exaggerated the story. It was said that EIGHT empty coffins had been found.

This news incensed the townspeople still more and a huge crowd marched to the Moss. The empty coffin was mounted shoulder-high and carried into town by the mob, who had armed themselves with iron railings and fencing stobs. The magistrates confronted them at Glen Lane. There, a goodly number backed off, but the remainder stoned the police!

After breaking the windows of the town's medical men, the rioters made their way to 'breathe vengeance' on the Oakshaw Cholera Hospital. They smashed the windows and gained entrance to the medical room, hoping to find a doctor. Instead, they found a jar of whisky and were soon fighting drunk. The cholera van was seized and carried at the head of a procession through the town. The angry mob threw the van into the Paisley Canal. As the rioters arrived at the Paisley Cross, they were confronted by the militia with guns at the ready. However, by this time the crowd's drunken anger had cooled and the militia held their fire. The crowd finally dispersed.

The local authority issued handbills offering a reward of £50 for the capture of the 'body snatchers'. None were found. However, as a precaution, the next day a watch was maintained over the burial ground at the Moss. The fears of the rioters, who thought the doctors were stealing the dead bodies for medical research, were allayed to some degree.

The cholera epidemic affected 769 persons, of whom 446 died. The dreadful disease had thrown Paisley into a panic. Death had knocked on every door, rich and poor alike. There was no escape. All the measures taken in combating the disease were of "a remedial or curative nature". No mention was made of looking for the cause and the disease returned to Paisley in 1854. This time fifty people died. The epidemics only ceased when, finally, sanitary conditions improved.

In the leafy enclave of Oakshaw Street, Hutcheson's Charity School appears on the right. During the Cholera epidemic, this was converted into the Oakshaw Cholera Hospital. (photo:courtesy Paisley Museum)

The John Neilson Institution

"The Porridge Bowl"

The profiles of the buildings on Oakshaw Hill give Paisley one of the finest skylines in Scotland. Towering above one end of this remarkable skyline is the old school building with its wonderful dome, still affectionately known in Paisley as the "Porridge Bowl". This elegant, classical building, designed in the form of a Greek Cross, was, until a few years ago, the John Neilson Institution, one of Paisley's best-known schools.

Not so long ago, when the newly maroon-blazered pupils hurried up the steep slopes of West Brae to attend school, one of the first lessons they were taught was how to spell the founder's name properly. The rector liked to tell new pupils, "It's Neilson... Nelson lost an eye, but Neilson never did!" So who was this John Neilson?

John Neilson was born in Paisley on December 14th, 1778. He had an elder brother James and three younger sisters, Marion, Mary and Jean. It was thought that when the two brothers, James and John, were young, they either attended

The old school badge.

the Grammar School in School Wynd or the Low Parish School in Storie Street.

Their father, John Neilson, ran a successful grocer's shop at Paisley Cross. When his two sons completed their education, they became apprenticed to their father in the grocery business. By 1811, James and John were made partners in the family shop, operating as John Neilson & Sons. Over the years their grocery business thrived, despite the economic ups and downs that the town suffered. Good management and the thrifty nature of the Neilsons saw them through hard times. After the death of his father and then his elder brother, John Neilson continued to run the shop profitably for many years.

However, in 1833, all this was to suddenly change. A disastrous fire ravaged Paisley Cross. John Neilson 's shop and his house above it fell prey to the flames. Fortunately, John had put aside a considerable fortune for such a rainy day. Throughout his bachelor life, he had been very thrifty. A contemporary of his, Walter McGibbon a Paisley joiner, recalled just how thrifty John Neilson really was. He remembered, "John Neilson of the Big School was always standing waiting to be bought a drink, but rarely returned the compliment." John Neilson had better things to do with his money. He purchased Nethercommon Estate and retired to live in its large mansion. He died there in 1839, aged 61, and was buried in Paisley Abbey.

Three months before his death, John Neilson signed a trust deed settlement in which a considerable part of his wealth, £18,000, was to be used to "form and endow" a school. It was to be for the education and maintenance of boys who had lived in Paisley for three years and whose parents were either dead, or unable

The old school's F.P. badge, used between 1881-1989.

to afford education. No one really knows why Neilson became interested in education, but the influence and suggestions of his nephew Archibald Gardner may have persuaded his uncle to found a school. Gardner, who was a lawyer, was one of the main trustees of the school and, for many years, his portrait gazed benevolently on the pupils gathered in the assembly hall.

The new school was opened on 5th April, 1852, as the John Neilson Educational Institution. Charles Wilson, who was the leading Glasgow architect of the day, designed this outstanding building with its well-proportioned frontage in a modern Renaissance style. A lofty portico led to the imposing entrance and a truncated cupola or dome soared upward to the skies

On the opening day, a sheet of printed instructions was issued, "to be strictly observed by every pupil" of the new school. Some rules mentioned were:

Obedience and respect are to be given to the teachers.

No pupil is to be absent without leave.

No pupils must touch the plants, trees or flowers.

No pupils must disfigure the buildings.

No stones must be thrown within the school precincts.

Another strictly-observed rule was also issued concerning the dangers of fire, as John Neilson had never forgotten how his grocer's shop had been so quickly comsumed.

PUPILS ARE NOT ALLOWED TO CARRY LUCIFER MATCHES, GUNPOWDER OR FIREARMS.

The final stricture was, "Pupils are strictly prohibited from the use of tobacco in any shape or form."!

By the 1870's, the school had established an educational record second to none. One school inspector reported, "This school is one of the very few educational triumphs we have in Scotland. In an excellent situation, it is surrounded by ample and well-laid out playgrounds. The premises are large, handsome and, in every detail, thoroughly adapted to school-work. The infant department is far the best I have seen in Scotland".

The school maintained these high standards well into the 20th Century and even won a medal at the Paris Exhibition of 1901 for its educational exhibit. The old school has produced a plethora of famous 'old boys', Captain A. Henderson V. C., Thomas Tait the famous architect, Jimmy Cowan Scotland's greatest goalkeeper, Kenneth McKellar the world-famous tenor, Gordon Williams the novelist and author of "Straw Dogs", Crawford Fairbrother MBE. Champion British High Jumper, Sandy Stoddart the classical sculptor and many, many more.

Former pupils have fond memories of the old school... of climbing the West Brae shouting "Up the Neilie Toosh!"... of toiling up the spiral staircase to the top of the dome (a privilege granted on a pupil's last day at school)... of the many characters on the teaching staff, Puddles, Kewie, Teenie, Gabbie, Madge and Tony Curtis to name a few.

In 1968, the "Porridge Bowl" closed its doors for the last time and moved to new premises at Millarston. The old building was converted to flats and the former assembly hall is graced by a fine statue created by Sandy Stoddart.

John Urie, photographer

John Urie. (1820-1910)

John Urie was born in Paisley in 1820. His father, a silk hand-loom weaver, owned a cottage in Wellmeadow Street, where he ran a six-loom weaving shop. This modest business made him one of Paisley's 'Sma corks'.

At an early age, John attended "Wee Willie Aitken's" school in nearby Castle Street. There, he was taught the three 'R's' and introduced to drawing, painting and even astronomy, Aitken's speciality. After attending classes for only six weeks, John became a draw-boy in his father's weaving shop. He was set to the loom, making shawl fringes. John disliked this work and got a job serving in his cousin's tavern in Glasgow, where he dispensed drams and picked up Glasgow slang from some of the rough customers. When his father heard about this, he insisted that his son come back to Paisley, to learn a decent, respectable trade. Young John became an apprentice stereotyper with Paisley's leading printer/publisher, John Neilson. He made type for Neilson for four years, but left over a dispute in wages. Now aged 22 and with some experience behind him, John left Paisley and set up his own business in Glasgow's Gallowgate, making large wooden type for use in bills and posters.

As a naturally skilled draughtsman, it was easy for John to turn his hand to wood engraving. He was asked to make an engraving showing the public execution of two Glasgow murderers, Doolan & Redding. He made a quick sketch of the public gibbet the day before the executions and added in the figures of the condemned men. He then printed broadsheets to sell at one penny each. On the day of execution, John sold thousands of copies to eager spectators and made a handsome profit.

NEW PHOTOGRAPHIC PORTRAITS ON GLASS,
33 BUCHANAN STREET, GLASGOW.

THE immense superiority of Collodionized Glass Pictures in comparison with ordinary Daguerreotypes or Calotypes, whether for portraits or still life, has already been acknowledged by the most eminent scientific men. With the view of introducing this beautiful class of art to the notice of the public, JOHN URIE has, for a considerable time, devoted his attention to the advancement of the process. Having succeeded in perfecting several improvements in it, J. Urie begs to announce that he is now prepared to execute Portraits on every variety of scale, as well as the Copying or Reduction of Pictures, and natural objects of all kinds. Examples of various classes may be seen in J. Urie's Studio, 33 Buchanan Street. The Prices range from 2s 6d upwards.

JOHN URIE,
PHOTOGRAPHIC PORTRAIT ROOMS,
33 BUCHANAN STREET.

A Urie advert of the late 1850s informing his public
that he was up to date in the latest advances in photography.

In his social life, he knew people like William Miller the author of "Wee Willie Winkie". Years later, the subject of this famous poem became one of John Urie's apprentices!

In 1849, he moved his office to Buchanan Street, where he made wood engravings for the "Practical Mechanics" monthly magazine.

He visited the Great Exhibition of 1851 in London, where the machinery and photographs displayed were the 'principal sources of attraction to him'. On one visit, he saw the Duke of Wellington on horseback. John recognised him at once and doffed his hat. The Duke instantly returned the salute!

When he returned to Glasgow, John Urie took up photography, making his first camera out of an old cigar box with the lens made from old spectacles. In the attic space of his office, he built a glasshouse studio, one of the earliest in Glasgow. Soon, the public were clamouring for their portraits. Such was his success in this new-fangled art, that, in 1852, he exhibited his portraits at the Johnstone Mechanics' Institute. His clientele gradually built up and was to include the Duke of Montrose, Betty Burns the poet's daughter, David Livingstone the African explorer, Dr James 'Paraffin' Young, John Robertson

Urie's portrait of his friend Dr David Livingstone, the famous African explorer.

engineer of the 'Comet' steamship and many other celebrities. David Livingstone and Urie became friends. Livingstone visited the studio several times to receive lessons in photography from Urie and proved an apt pupil.

One of Urie's most notorious clients was a young lady of good birth and breeding, whose deeds were soon to startle the world. Three months after her portrait was taken, this strikingly beautiful young girl was put on trial for murder. Her name was Madeleine Smith.

Madeleine stood accused of the murder of her lover, Émile L'Angelier, by arsenic poisoning. In 1857, during the trial, Urie displayed a large hand-tinted photograph of her in his shop window. His shop was beseiged with onlookers, such was the public interest in one of Scotland's most sensational trials. Urie was asked by the police to remove the portrait, but refused to do so. The publicity given to his studio was too good to miss!

Another person Urie met socially was the infamous Glasgow murderer, Dr Pritchard. Urie thought him an odd character and fortunately did not befriend him. He also knew a fellow photographer called John Greatex , who became infamous as a forger of banknotes. Strange acquaintances for a respectable Paisley man!

John Urie died in 1910. He is best remembered for his portraits of the famous and infamous persons of his time. His pioneer work in photography included the invention, in the 1850s, of a clockwork machine which could develop and print pictures at the rate of 100 copies an hour. John Urie's machine was not a great commercial success. but he had the satisfaction of knowing that it paved the way towards the birth of cinematography.

Advert on back of a Urie carte-de- visite. Urie had been awarded Royal Letters Patent for his improvements in photography.

John Urie was born in 1820 in Well meadow, where his father ran a six loom weaving shop. Wellmeadow appears in the centre of the picture with Sandholes to the left.

Dr Pritchard, the infamous Glasgow murderer. Urie met him socially, but did not dare befriend him!

Urie's portrait of Betty Burns, the daughter of the poet, Robert Burns.

James Fillans

Self -portrait of James Fillans, made in 1835 while he was a
young man studying art in Paris.

Early in the 19th Centuty, James Fillans came to reside and work in Paisley with his family. His father opened a small grocery shop and the teenaged James was apprenticed to the loom. In his leisure hours, James, an artistic young man, took to designing things. He made a number of bird cages, some of them exceedingly elegant in construction. Young James' talent did not end there. He astonished his workmates by making a cage with a wheel turned by a real mouse. This was attached to a model loom, with a weaver carved in wood. As the mouse turned the wheel, the model actually worked. His automaton weaver working at the loom was exhibited in the window of the family home. This attracted a great deal of attention from the admiring public. After this, the boys in the neighbourhood dubbed young James the "mouse genius! "

In Paisley, at one of the many clay holes, young James found a ready source of clay. To the amazement and delight of his friends, the clay took living shapes in James' hands. Of the many animal forms he created, he regarded his elephant as his first masterpiece. These were his first real attempts at sculpture.

This sculptured marbled slab modelled by Fillans was presented to Dr James Kerr in 1840. Kerr was the gentleman responsible for giving Paisley its first supply of piped water in 1838. The medallion portrait of Kerr appears in the centre.

A story is told that, when James was only six years old, he made a clay helmet for his young brother John. He had been reading about the exploits of Sir William Wallace and decided to make "Wallace's helmet" for his brother. He prepared a quantity of clay, rolled it out, clapped on his brother's head, moistened it with water and modelled the headpiece much to his brother's annoyance!

Abandoning the loom to further his interest in sculpture, James took up the mallet and chisel as an apprentice stone mason with a local builder, McLatchie. During this period, he carved sculptures for various Paisley buildings. His first private commission was the sculpture of a horse designed to sit above a blacksmith's shop at Lonend. Older readers may remember this spirited work of great beauty which survived on the frontage of the old Gleniffer Soap Works at Lonend.

In 1828, when only twenty years old, James was employed in carving the interior Corinthian capitals at Glasgow's Royal Exchange (now the Museum of Modern Art) in Queen Street. This young, self-taught sculptor astonished his fellow masons with such facility in intricate carving that they called him "The Young Athens".

In 1835, William Motherwell, the well-known Paisley antiquarian and poet, and other locals encouraged James to set up his first studio in Paisley. There, his first professional commission was to execute a bust of Motherwell. Soon, others were clamouring for their portraits. His fine bust of the influential Sheriff Campbell added to his growing reputation as a sculptor.

He opened a studio in Glasgow's Miller Street. A contemporary said, "It was here that we first made his acquaintance. He was young strong and handsome, with a noble artistic head, somewhat grave and silent in his manner, but full of a deep poetic enthusiasm for his art". Commissions flowed in.

In 1848, Fillans was commisioned by his townsman to make a bust of one of Paisley's great literary sons, Professor John Wilson. When it was publicly unveiled in the town it was said that the bust was a masterpiece of art. It would long be prized by Paisley as a faithful likenesss of their gifted townsman and as a memorial of the genius of Mr Fillans.

In 1833, he married a Paisley girl, Grace Gemmell. Two years later, he took leave of his wife to go on a 'Grand Tour', taking in London and Paris.

Such were the commissions he received in London, that he decided to open a studio there.

Once again, the commissions rolled in. To bring him notice in the capital, he exhibited seven busts at the Royal Academy, where Chantrey, Britain's leading sculptor, paid him the highest praise. Although he now had a studio in London, Fillans resided mainly in Scotland and carried out a number of local commissions. One that can still seen is the magnificent, delicately-carved monument to Dr Kerr in Woodside Cemetery, based on his earlier testimonial. Dr Kerr was the man who was responsible for giving Paisley its first piped water supply.

Paisley honoured the now famous Fillans with a public dinner in 1844. Homage was paid to this great man of genius by all the leading townspeople.

His fine bust of Professor John Wilson (Christopher North), his fellow townsman, was completed in 1848. It was described at its unveiling in Paisley as "the most striking likeness possible and indeed is a masterpiece of art". This bust is now in Paisley Museum.

In 1851, Fillans closed his expensive London studio to concentrate on his domestic life and busy studio in Glasgow. But this was not to be. He died in 1852 aged forty-four. It appears that the long hours in damp studios and the mental and physical labour involved in his noble profession had caught up with him.

The marble monument "Rachel Weeping for her Children", which he had designed for the tomb of his father, marks his own last resting place. It can be seen at Woodside Cemetery. It stands as a testimony, along with his other works, to a man of rare genius of whom Paisley can be proud.

The marble statue "Rachel Weeping for her Children"
which marks the tomb of the sculptor at Woodside Cemetery.

The early life of James Clark

James Clark I. (1747-1829) who set up business at 10 Cotton St. as a weaver's finisher, heddle twine-maker and thread manufacturer

The history of the cotton spool trade in Paisley is synonomous with the Clark family. In 1753, William Clark, a farmer at Dykebar, died leaving a large family. Too young to work the farm, his children took employment in nearby Paisley. One son, James Clark, set up business at 10 Cotton Street as a humble weaver and, through time, became a weaver's furnisher and heddle twine- maker and then a thread manufacturer.

In a thatched cottage in Cotton Street, James and his wife raised a family of fourteen children. In 1783, his fifth child was born and named for his father. Young James' early years were undistinguished. He received a meagre instruction in reading, writing and arithmetic, usually from his older siblings. His father could spare little time from his labours, yet James "entertained the strongest feelings of reverence and affection" for him.

At the tender age of seven, James became a draw-boy in his father's six-loom shop, the first step in becoming a weaver. He was a shy and timid boy. Because of this, his older shopmates treated him roughly and, for some reason or other, gave him the nickname of "Tuppence". But, when his father appeared in the workshop, James found in him "a safe asylum" and a kind master.

One of the irksome tasks assigned to young James was to help his father in the manufacture of heddles. James even worked on Saturdays, when other children went for country jaunts. James often complained to his parents that he was denied such health-giving pleasures. However, as time passed, help came, when his second sister, Margaret, was given the task of making heddles, leaving James free to enjoy the pleasures of life.

James was brought up by his father to give particular attention to economy and propriety, reflecting the hard times the Clark family had experienced. Young James was first dressed in a pair of 'calches'. This article of clothing combined trousers, vest and jacket in one. This was all his wardrobe, shoes he had none. A

James Clark II (1783-1865) Born and reared at 10 Cotton St. where he was an apprentice weaver to his father. In later life he became known as James Clark of Chapel House and, with his brother John, founded the huge firm of thread makers J & J Clark at the Seedhill Mills.

hat or bonnet was out of the question.

When he had grown a little, James managed to save 1/6d and bought his first bonnet, which he wore to attend church. On his way home, he was caught in a shower of rain, so he took off the bonnet and tucked it under his arm. When he arrived home, disaster struck. While his sister was trimming an oil lamp, she spilled a large quantity of oil on the cherished bonnet and ruined it! He ran to his mother with heavy heart and complained that he would never be able to afford another. "Tut" said his mother, "Thou surely don't think that eighteen pence is an insurmountable obstacle in gaining a new head dress?"

By dint of hard work, James eventually became a fully-fledged weaver. In the six-loomed weaving shop, he worked beside his eldest brother, William, and his younger brother, Andrew. One of the journeyman weavers was Alexander Wilson, who was to become famous as a poet and ornithologist. As James worked beside him, he noticed that Wilson was seldom seen without a book or writing material, "jotting down his fancies as they flitted past his well-stored, original mind". Wilson fell in love with one of the Clark sisters, but fortune did not favour him!

Although James was fond of company, he also enjoyed homely pursuits. He was fond of cultivating flowers in a small part of the kailyard, at the back of the weaving shop. In the neighbouring garden, the tenant kept hens. These became a continual source of annoyance to James, as they raided his cherished flower garden, scratching and digging in the search for worms. James declared war on the hens and always kept a good supply of stones at the ready, to repel the invaders. One day, as the hens retreated through a hole in the hedge, James aimed a stone. To his horror, the stone broke one of the hen's legs. James ran to the house and confessed all to his mischievous brother Andrew, who was usually blamed for all the mishaps in the Clark household. When the irate neighbour called in to the Clark household, she naturally thought Andrew was the culprit

The vast complex of Clark's Mills expanded over the years to gigantic proportions. This aerial view was taken of the whole complex in 1930.

and accused him, shouting, "What for did you break ma hen's leg?" James was never accused and so got off Scot-free! Such were the scenes in the early Clark household in Cotton Street.

At the age of 21, James "espoused Margaret Campbell", then a girl of seventeen, and "commenced in earnest the rough journey of life". Soon, with care and saving, he built a house at Seedhill. When the last straw was put upon the roof and the final shilling paid, James recalled this time as the happiest days of his life. The little building served as a lodging and workshop and, in later years, became the cradle of Paisley's thread trade.

James and his brother John joined their father in the manufacture of smooth fine cotton, originally designed to replace the silk used in the heddles for the looms. In 1819, the two brothers formed the firm of J &J Clark and took over their father's mill at Seedhill. James was now a prosperous mill owner, a property owner and a public figure in Paisley. He moved to a large house in Ardgowan Brae called Chapel House. So, from heddles and hens, bobbins and bonnets, James Clark had come a long way from his poor, humble beginnings in Cotton Street. He died in 1865.

David Stow

David Stow. (1793-1864) The genius of classroom and chalkface.

Most school teachers in Paisley realise that their summer holidays are nearly over when they see posters in shop windows bearing the ominous words "Back to School". Parents usually welcome the signs!

All Scottish children now have the benefit of education, but it was not always so. Education was not generally provided for the poorest children and teaching standards were very varied. As in so many other spheres, it was a Paisley man who paved the way. His name was David Stow and he did indeed help to ensure that all children would get "Back to School".

This genius of classroom and chalkface was born into a prosperous family home in Stow Place, on 17th May, 1793. A plaque in nearby Causeyside, records his birthplace.

NEAR THIS SCHOOL,*
THE BENEFACTION OF HIS SISTER ELIZABETH STOW,
WAS BORN 17TH MAY 1793,
DAVID STOW,
AUTHOR OF THE "TRAINING SYSTEM OF EDUCATION," AND
FOUNDER OF THE FIRST BRITISH TRAINING COLLEGES FOR
TEACHERS.
ERECTED BY THE RENFREWSHIRE LOCAL
ASSOCIATION AT PAISLEY STOW CENTENARY CONGRESS
OF EDUCATIONAL INSTITUTE OF SCOTLAND 1893.
*REMOVED 1903.

Plaque which was removed from above the doorpiece of the old Stow School in Causeyside and incorporated into the wall of the tenement built on the site of the old school.

After receiving a classical education at Paisley Grammar School, Stow entered the commercial world of Glasgow 'counting houses' in 1811. There, he was appalled by the disease-ridden, overcrowded conditions of the city's poor children and by their lack of education.

Coming from a religious background, he became a Sabbbath school teacher in Glasgow's Tron Church. There he taught children the rudiments of the Christian faith and a little reading and writing. To recruit pupils for his Sabbath school, he wandered through the dangerous, disease-ridden, dark wynds of the Saltmarket.

Stow described these forays as "deep sea fishing". He advised his fellow church elders canvassing for pupils in other parts of the city, "Don't go with a paper in your hand, the people will have the idea that you are collecting taxes"!

The Sabbath school could not cope with such large numbers of "dissolute and corrupted children", so David Stow opened a day infant school for boys and girls aged under six. By 1826, he had founded the Glasgow Infant School Society. One year later, he opened another school in the Drygait of Glasgow.

This city school was innovative. As well as providing pupils with an atmosphere conducive to learning, it had a playground! This, Stow described as an "uncovered classroom". The idea of a city school having a playground was regarded by his contemporaries as totally eccentric!

Stow pioneered the idea that each school should have a playground.
This he described as an "uncovered classroom".

Stow was ahead of his time. At his school the concept of "picturing out" the lessons was first used. Nowadays all teachers use visual aids in their lessons. His other innovations included co-education of both sexes, the abolition of corporal punishment and the abolition of prize-givings.

Word spread of his school's success. One famous visitor, Robert Owen (pioneer of New Lanark Mills), was moved to tears when he saw poor children being taught so well. He was amazed how easily the children learned their lessons. Soon, student teachers flocked to this school, to learn about Stow's new teaching methods.

In 1828, Stow published his first book "Teacher Training" which brought him national acclaim. Despite his success, the early years of his married life, were marred when his first son almost died from "inflammation of the lungs". Then his wife, Marion, died in 1831, from what Stow described as "malignant fever".

In 1833, Stow published another book with the strange title "Granny and Leezy", in which "Granny" represented the old, out-dated method of education and "Leezy", Stow's ideals of teaching and training.

One year later, he published "Moral Training for Large Cities" which laid out the principles of his teaching methods and became widely adopted.

In November, 1836, David Stow laid the foundation stone of his Normal Training Seminary in Cowcaddens (the Normal School). This alone created

Stow's Free Church Normal Seminary Glasgow in 1854.

education history, as it was the first purpose-built teacher training college in Great Britain. The hallmarks of the college were its strict entrance exams and the weekly "crits" (criticisms) when student teachers taught their classes in front of their tutors.

Alas, all Stow's work in building up his college suffered a major blow when, in 1838, a Treasury grant of £1,000 was required to wipe out the college's debts. Stow, a fiercely independent man, had to allow a take-over of the college by the Church of Scotland. Unless he did this, no further government money was to be forthcoming.

His new masters, the Church of Scotland, decreed that the college be restricted to members of their church. This was contrary to Stow's philosophy. As he was a supporter of the Free Church, he believed in inter-denominational study and co-operation. In 1845, matters came to a head and he was forced to withdraw from the college he had founded for the whole community.

Within a month of marching out of the college with his enthusiastic followers, Stow set up tents on another site in Glasgow. There, under canvas, the Normal Seminary went back to work. This great publicity stunt had its rewards, for he was soon laying another foundation stone, on this site, for the Free Church Seminary! Stow had proved his point. The new building was a great success and had government funding!

The Stow St. School Paisley situated at Causeyside / Stow St. junction. The school was run for many years by Stow's sister, Elizabeth, who left it to the town. The building was demolished in 1903 to be replaced by the present day tenement.

Again, personal tragedy struck Stow. His second marriage lasted only six years when his wife died. This was followed by the death of two of his sons.

Stow never got over his family losses. He himself died in 1864, aged 71, at Bridge of Allan. However, his ideas had grown to command great respect in the world of education. He had been a pioneer and had made education history. His famous dictum "Train up a child in the way he should go and when he is old, he will not depart from it." is still valid today. Marble busts of the great educationalist can be seen at Kelvingrove Museum and appropriately at Jordanhill Teacher Training College. Part of the Jordanhill Campus is called the David Stow Building. Stow College in Glasgow is also called after this son of Paisley.

Rowan Street

Neilston Road / Rowan Street corner in 1870.
These once elegant 18th Century buildings formed part of Dovesland, but became slums through neglect in the Victorian age. The Dooslan' Stane sits at the corner

When 'city slickers' come from Glasgow to Paisley for the first time, whether on business or pleasure, they usually get lost. The Glasgow 'keelies' are truly surprised by just how big is the town of Paisley.

Over the centuries, Paisley's busy streets have given shape and dimension to the town and formed an intricate Paisley Pattern of a different order. In what other Scottish town could you find streets named Cotton, Silk, Gauze, Incle, Shuttle and Thread?

Each was named to reflect our former glory in the textile trade. Paisley's past historians have written reams about how such and such a street got its name. In some cases, even they, too, have become 'lost' in the welter of old names. Take, for example, Rowan Street in Paisley's South-End. Metcalfe in his "History of Paisley" said it was called after the rowan tree. Nothing could be farther from the truth!

In 18th Century Paisley, Robert Rowan (or Rowand - spelling was not yet standardised) was well- known as the Laird of Dovesland and Kilncroft. Rowan Street was named after him. In 1782, he is mentioned as one of the sundry

Duke Street which branched off Rowan Street formed part of the properties owned by the Rowan family. Through time and neglect, these houses fell into sad disrepair and became unfit for human habitation, and were eventually demolished.

owners of land in Paisley. "Adjoining the lands of Lylesland, lie the lands of Dovesland and Kilncroft, the property owned by Mr Robert Rowand".

Over the years, Robert Rowand developed and owned all the properties on both sides of Duke Street and Rowan Street. The latter street cut through his extensive property. To the north was Dovesland, the original home to Paisley's Dooslan Stane, and to the south the lands of Kilncroft, now partly occupied by the South Primary School. Kilncroft was once the place where limestone taken from the nearby 'crags', was burned in kilns and turned into lime.

In 1850, Robert's daughter, Mary Rowan of Dovesland, who had fallen heir to her father's extensive properties in Rowan Street, took court action against local starch manufacturers, Messrs Brown & Polson. At that time, their factory was situated in Thrushcraigs, further up Rowan Street. Because Brown & Polson had taken it upon themselves to repair the road fronting her houses in Rowan Street, Mary claimed that this work had encroached on her private property and that she was the owner of the road.

After a long tedious proof by Mary Rowan's lawyers, it was found that the road in question was a public thoroughfare and had been in existence for a least a hundred years previously. It was ruled that Brown & Polson had every right to repair the road. Mary Rowan lost her case.

REPORT OF CASE

MARY ROWAN, OF DOVESLAND,

against

Messrs. BROWN & POLSON,

STARCH MANUFACTURERS, THRUSHCRAIG.

Out of which arises the

HISTORY OF THE LANDS

OF

BLACKHALL AND THORNLEY

OF PAISLEY:

A newspaper cutting of 1850 detailing the court case between Mary Rowan of Dovesland and Messrs Brown & Polson, starch manufacturers.

Mary, who had married a Robert Caldwell, died in 1867 and left her property to her son, Robert Rowan Caldwell. He had become a minister in the Free Church of Scotland and was to have problems, more temporal than spiritual. When Robert inherited his mother's properties, the houses at Dovesland, Duke Street and Rowan Street had, over the years, become delapidated and totally unfit for human habitation.

What had once been the desirable rented homes of the handloom weavers of Charleston were now occupied by humble bleachfield workers and the poorest of the labouring classes.

Three of the houses still had thatched roofs, no uncommon sight in Victorian Paisley. One of these had been a but-and-ben, with half used as a stable. Abutting another house was a piggery. All the houses had earth floors and walls saturated with damp to ceiling level. There was no sign of a toilet anywhere. An open gutter in front of the houses was used to dump all kinds of slop and filth. The poor tenants had to sleep in damp box-beds. The foul-smelling sinks had no running water.

All in all, there were about 40 houses in such appalling condition. When the owner, Rev. Caldwell, was approached by the sanitary authorities to make much needed improvements for his tenants, he resented their interference and demands. The reverend gentleman even appealed by letter to the local authority, but they backed their sanitary inspector's findings. The minister was still so objurate that court proceedings were authorised against him. He could fulfil their demands or be taken to law.

A few days later, the minister appeared to relent and arranged a meeting with the sanitary inspector on site. At the meeting, the minister advanced all the well-worn arguments in defence of his properties, some of which were "quite ridiculous for the time". They seemed even more cruel when uttered by a minister of the gospel. He argued that he was conferring a benefit and a blessing, in offering a cheap class of houses to those poor people!

Finally, the patience of the sanitary inspector ran out. He turned on the minister and in a quiet, emotive voice said, "Sir, you are a minister of the Lord

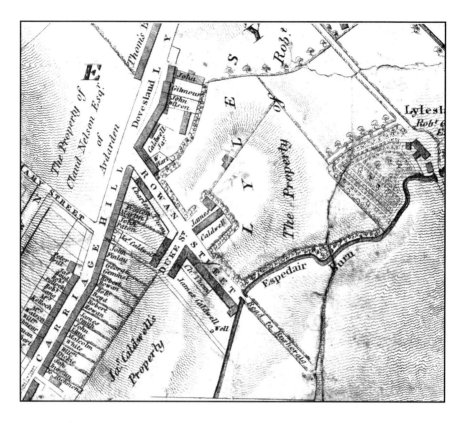

A map of Rowan Street in 1822. Notice the sundry owners' names, set against each property. These include the Rowans, the Caldwells and Charles Thom, the speculative builder who gave his name to Charleston in Paisley's South End.

whose mission is to preach the gospel of 'Peace on earth, goodwill to all men'. I ask you is it possible under these cicumstances to do unto others as you would that others do to you?" This argument seemed to prick the conscience of the minister and, within two days, the necessary undertakings were made. The three hovels in Dovesland were closed up and the large scheme of sanitary improvements implemented at the others.

The old tenements in Rowan Street at Dovesland were finally demolished around 1896. Paisley people will remember the vacant Duke Street site, which was the location of an annual visit of 'The Shows'.

The only remains of old Dovesland are the local fish and chip shop in Neilston Road and the Dooslan' Stane now resting in Brodie Park.

Robert Brown

92

Doon the Watter

A crowd of eminent Paisley men aboard the steamship Gleniffer as she passes under the old Inchinnan Bridge on her last trip "Doon the Watter".

In the early 1830s, Paisley Buddies who wished to treat themselves to a sail 'doon the watter' to Gourock or Largs had to make their way to a pick-up point at some distance from Paisley. They would board the Glasgow passenger steamer as it called in at the 'Water Neb', the junction of the Cart and Clyde at Inchinnan.

One enterprising family, the Robertsons who owned a public house in Paisley's Sneddon, soon had a thriving sideline in the boat trip trade. Old Willie Robertson and his two sons owned several small boats. These sailed down the River Cart from Sneddon Quay to the Water Neb, loaded with passengers to meet the Glasgow steamer. Robertson's young sons, Willie and Tammie, rowed the small boats. They were kind, courteous and obliging to their paying passengers and were well-liked in Paisley.

Trade at this time was good and many Paisley people took the opportunity of 'visiting the salt water'. However, it soon became apparent that Robertsons' boats were too small and too few to meet the popular demand and a small steam boat from Glasgow was brought in to sail directly from the Sneddon Quay to the coastal resorts. The name of this vessel was the "Cupid". She proved to be unreliable. Very often she would break down, leaving the Paisley passengers stranded. Such was her reputation that the local wags called her "Stupid".

In 1838 the Royal Victoria Steamship made her maiden voyage "Doon the Watter". She was built at Abercorn Foundry by Messrs Barr & McNab who invited a discerning public to sample the splendid and comfortable cabins of their powerful new steam packet. (picture:courtesy Dr S. Clark)

In 1834, the Cupid was replaced by another boat, the "Gleniffer", named after Paisley's Gleniffer Braes. She was larger and finer than her predecessor and, although only weighing 32 tons, was nimble enough to negotiate the narrow banks of the River Cart. She soon became the pride of the town. As the Gleniffer steamed her way to Greenock and Gourock she would be packed with Paisley trippers. Greenock folk could no longer taunt their Paisley neighbours that Paisley was a town full of landlubbers! Many a tradesman and his wife went sailing down the Clyde to enjoy the sea breezes and to "encourage their ain shipping" from the harbour at Paisley.

The Gleniffer sailed from the Sneddon on Saturdays at full tide and dropped her passengers off at Port Glasgow, Greenock and Gourock. She would return on Mondays, with her Paisley passengers eager to tell their neighbours what wonderful sights they had seen. Even to see sand and gather sea-shells was a novelty in those days.

The ship's safe return to the Sneddon was eagerly awaited by one man in particular. Old Willie Robertson would constantly look down the River Cart until he saw smoke appearing at the river bend. At this sight, he became overjoyed. He would cry to the crowds gathered at the quay side, "Stand back, weans! Stand back, callans! There she comes with her glorious cargo."

One of old Willie's duties was to supply the Gleniffer with ' three cairts o' coal'. He would carefully break up the bigger lumps of coal and throw water over them "to mak' them last longer"! At the same time, he would warn the crowds of children gathered at the quay, "Don't throw the coal in the Cart!"

One old Paisley lady made her first voyage from Cart to Clyde. As she stood on the deck, she overheard a conversation between the helmsman and a passenger. The passenger had asked why there were so many brightly painted casks floating in the Clyde. "These are buoys to mark the course for vessels.", the helmsman replied. The old Paisley lady became so excited on hearing the word

CARLILE QUAY.

Carlile Quay in the Sneddon became a hive of activity with the arrival and departure of the SS Gleniffer and the SS Royal Victoria. To go "Doon the Watter" in the old days and sampling aquatic travel, possibly for the first time, was the trip of a lifetime.

'buoy' that she approached the captain shouting, "Save us! What can a boy be doing out there? He'll be drowned, he's somebody's bairn. Oh, man, haud up the handle o' your boat, let aff steam, and tak' him up."

During 1834, the number of passengers eager to have their first trip Doon the watter on board the Gleniffer had reached twelve thousand. The vessel was to ply between the waters of the Cart and the Clyde for many years, until she was finally sold to a company in Dartmouth in 1863. Sadly, she never reached her new home. In her voyage south, the old ship hit rocks near Penzance and was wrecked. Fortunately, all on board were saved.

In 1838, the "Royal Victoria" was the first steamship built and launched in Paisley. She began her work in sailing down the Clyde from the Sneddon. Her captain, Archie McGill, had great difficulty in navigating her up the Cart owing to the shallowness of the water. As the steamer grounded on one bank after another, Archie would "claw at his elbow with his face aglow with rage". He would look at the man at the helm and shout, "Can ye no keep her oot o' they damned hedges?"

On one occasion when she was coming up the Clyde, the Royal Victoria had to pass a steamer sailing to Liverpool. The passengers on this large ship jeered those on board the much smaller, Paisley-built ship. This displeased the Paisley Buddies very much and one of them remarked in quite a rage, "What right had they to put straws doon oor funnel? " This remark became part of the local 'patter' meaning "to spoil our fun".

However, the Liverpool crowd who mocked the sturdy little steamship owed a debt to Paisley. After all, the honour of building the first iron ships belongs to the shipyards of the River Cart.

The Troglodyte Club

The annual outing of the Troglodyte Club in 1867. Members carefully pose in front of the Clochoderick Stone, near Lochwinnoch, to have their picture taken. (photo:courtesy Paisley Museum)

The town of Paisley was, and still is, strongly club-conscious. Most of the town's present-day clubs, such as the Burns Club and the Bohemian Club, are firmly rooted in Paisley's past.

Of the many drinking clubs prevalent in 19th Century Paisley, only names have survived. We once had the Baron Club, The Linn, The Pickled Inglan Club and many others, but the most aptly named was the Troglodyte Club.

In the Troglodyte Club, which was founded around 1857, the discussion of literature went hand in hand with conviviality. Its founder Peter Tannahill, a nephew of Paisley's famous weaver poet Robert Tannahill, had been unfortunate in his business as a "Causeyside Cork". To reverse his fortunes, he became the

The Terrace Tavern, the underground howff of the Troglodytes appears behind and below the bridge at Paisley Cross. The pub's windows overlook the River Cart. The area over the river is now covered over by the Paisley Piazza.

landlord of the Terrace Tavern. This drinking howff was an underground vault built on the banks of the River Cart, next to the bridge at Paisley Cross. Its arched stone windows peered out just above the water level of the river. It was dark and dank, so the locals dubbed the tavern "The Hole". As it was so deeply set in the bowels of the earth and resembled a cave, the members who met there called themselves the "Troglodytes", or cave-dwellers.

The club was patronised by a number of old friends of the landlord. The membership was made up of ex-provosts, baillies and councillors of the burgh. Other members included lawyers, doctors, authors, newspaper editors, poets and painters. There, they drank beer, toddy and grog, indulged in cigars, pipes and tobacco and discussed literature, philosophy and the politics of the day.

THE ANNUAL

TROGLODYTE SUPPER

TO BE HELD

IN THE TERRACE TAVERN

On *THURSDAY 1st September 1870,*

At Half-past Eight p.m.

TICKET—TWO SHILLINGS AND SIXPENCE.

No. *21*   *W.G.*

An invitation card inviting members to the Annual Troglodyte Supper of 1870.
(picture:courtesy D.Malcolm)

When new members were elected to the club, they were expected to stand "Daunie's Roun". In typical Paisley fashion, they had to buy the first round of drinks! This was followed by the singing of the club song "The lass of Loanen", about a wee lassie living at Lonend, called Gussie,

"An tho' she's aft saucy, an flirts wi' the men,

She lo'es only me, sae I let her alane".

So many oysters were consumed at their meetings, that the club was dubbed the "Oyster Club". Such was the popularity of oysters on the menu, that several members decided to form a limited company to be called the "West of Scotland Oyster and General Fishery Company". It had a capital of £2,500 in 2500 shares of £1 each. At the time "it was not doubted that the company would grow to be a large and important undertaking". However, this ambitious business venture failed for these optimistic Paisley landlubbers.

Another disappointing failure for the club took place in 1872. The famous African explorer, Sir Henry Morton Stanley, had visited the town in October that year and captivated his Paisley audience in his lecture "How I Found Livingstone". Thinking themselves to be no small beer, the Troglodytes invited him to their club to give him a congratulary address. Stanley, however, declined the honour of attending, offering the plea of a press of engagements.

98

William Stewart

Architect and poet William Stewart joined the merry ranks of the Troglodytes in 1874.

As was to be expected in this town of poets, each literary club appointed its "poet laureate". The Troglodytes were no exception and William Stewart received this honour in 1874. Although born in Glasgow, Stewart was for many years an architect in Paisley and was responsible for the design of the, East, West, North and South Schools. One of his poems describes a typical night with the Troglodytes.

"The club room held a merry crew,

An ilka neuk was packit fu',

A gaucy chiel, o' jovial air,

Wi ' flowin beard an' snaw white hair,

An ample bouk, weel filled the chair".

In 1874, the club celebrated the centenary of the birth of the poet Tannahill with lengthy odes written in his memory.

On another occasion, it was recorded that the Troglodyte chairman was "not a speaker or a singer", but he could dance! When he danced, the whole club was infected and danced in spite of itself! It must have been a spectacle to see some of Paisley's most revered and respected men dancing with each other, performing a Scotch reel or an Irish jig, or even a senior baillie dancing with a bald-pated justice of the peace!

Another distinguished member of the Troglodytes was the poet Andrew Park. He wrote the fine poem "Silent Love".

"No man e'er loved like me. When but a boy

Love was my solace and my only joy;

Its mystic influence fired my tender soul,

And held me captive in its soft control..."

The Terrace Tavern, home of the Troglodytes and the scene of many convivial evenings, is buried under the concrete of the Paisley Piazza.

Fulton of the Glen

William Fulton, Laird of Glenfield. One of the kindest men that Paisley produced.

As a young man, William Fulton worked as a weaver in the West End of Paisley. He had been brought up near Tannahill's birthplace in Castle Street and knew the poet well.

William's mother had trained her young son to have careful habits and early in his working life he managed to save three silver half-crowns which he kept in a kist. Next door to the shop where he was serving his time as a weaver was a baker's shop. Here, William noticed a beautiful young girl working happily away. He thought she had "all the charms of an angel ". The girl took ill and became so lame that she was no longer fit for her work. Her employers dismissed her and sent her packing, penniless, back to her home in Glasgow. Before she left, Willie approached her and told her to "Stand there for a few minutes and don't leave until I come back". Willie returned and gave her his life savings of three half-crowns. He even paid for a carriage to convey the girl back to Glasgow.

Years later, while Willie was doing business in Glasgow, he saw a lady and four young girls riding in an open carriage. He was astonished when he recognised that she was the young girl from the bakery whom had helped out many years ago. She had married well, gone to America and come home to Glasgow to have her four daughters privately educated. Her success story made Willie a happy man. He said it was "like a dream".

At one time, Willie thought that to be the owner of a fine big grey horse and a bleachfield cart would be the height of his ambition and when he married Miss Alexander from Kilmarnock, they both saved all they could towards his dream. Willie, who worked as a warper in a Paisley textile warehouse with a set wage, took on extra work in the evenings, keeping the books for a friend's business. The 7/6d a week extra he made was carefully saved and soon he had £60-00 in the bank.

One day, he was told that Glenfield Estate was on the market, either to let or for sale. Willie had always loved this area, but he replied, "I have only enough money to buy a horse and cart." However, he took on the lease and moved in with his family. Eventually, in 1850, through hard work and successful business

Glen House, Glenfield. Around 1859 William Fulton built this mansionhouse. The dam in the foreground formed part of the complex of his dyeing and finishing works nearby. The house is long gone, but the dam still forms part of the Glen Nature Trail.

dealings, he managed to buy the "Glen" from the trustees of Robert Barclay. He had raised himself from being the tenant to being the landlord.

Willie had once said that "If Glenfield were mine, all the people of Paisley would be at liberty to come and walk by the braes and glens as if it were their own." and now, as the Laird of Glenfield, he kept true to his word. He would frequently send his bleachfield carts in to Paisley and bring out a happy company of weavers or "Maister Corks" to spend a pleasant summer's day at the Glen. There, they would be regaled with curds and cream and be given a tour of the extensive landscaped gardens. They would make a pilgrimage to "Tannahill's Well" which the laird had erected in memory of his old friend, the poet Robert Tannahill.

Willie's generosity was a legend in his life time. A dirty-looking beggarman used to doss in one of the outhouses at the Glen. When Willie found out, he decided

Tannahill's Well was the first monument erected in Paisley by William Fulton in memory of his boyhood friend Robert Tannahill.

to make the beggar more comfortable by building him a bed and fireplace. The only condition made to the tramp was that he was to have a bath and a set of new clothes. Willie proposed handing him over to the women scourers at the factory to clean him up. The poor man gave Willie a strange look. "Weel, weel "said Willie, "I'll gie you to the men, but scoured you must be"!

Willie was the originator of "Glenfield Starch". It began as a by-product in his successful dyeing and bleaching works at Glenfield when he had some sago left over from the cloth processing. He made this into starch and patented his product. Soon it was advertised in the streets of Paisley by sticking labels on every shop window in Causeyside. Fulton's product became a national success. Even the Royal Laundry pronounced that "it was the finest starch ever used". The starch manufacturing side of the business grew and was handed over to Wotherspoon and Co. at Maxwellton.

William Fulton of the Glen had, from humble beginnings, become one of the most successful businessmen that the town produced. During his life, he was a noted benefactor, taking a great interest in the poorhouse and the local hospital. He was forever giving out money to old friends who had fallen on hard times, yet he never once made it public knowledge. Willie's life was said to be "free from black spots and full of sunshine." His life, which ended in 1868, could fill a volume of good deeds.

Soap & Sir John McCallum

Sir John McCallum MP.
known locally as "Honest John".

"Nothing makes the home so clean, bright and attractive as the liberal use of A1 SOAP POWDER". This was an advertising slogan familiar to every Paisley housewife. The claims were made by Isdale & McCallum, the well -known Paisley soap-makers.

Packets of "A1 soap powder" were used in most Paisley households at one time or another. The housewife would open the neatly-designed packet and after much searching among the soap powder, out would fall a small thimble, supposedly to act as a dispenser for the powder. The manufacturers claimed that only a tiny drop, a thimbleful, was needed to do the washing up! But the packet held another surprise.... the all-important soap powder coupon ! These were carefully put aside and saved for many a week, as they could be exchanged for all sorts of 'gifts'at the firm's red-brick office building in Rowan Street. Saturday mornings saw a queue of Paisley Buddies, eager to redeem their coupons.

Ironically, although Paisley was dubbed "The dirtiest town in Scotland.", in Victorian times, soap-making flourished in Paisley and had done so since the 18th Century. Soap was a necessary commodity, used by the weavers, bleachers, dyers and cloth finishers of a textile town like Paisley. Paisley could boast the oldest soapmakers business in Scotland, Wm Sim & Co. Other leading companies were John Bell, Oliver Jamieson, Robin & Houston, The Gleniffer Soap Co., and the St Mirren Soapworks.

However, the most successful of these companies was Isdale & McCallum. It became a household name throughout the British Empire, with its famous brands "Thistle"and "A1" soaps.

The founders of this illustrious company were Ralph Isdale and John Mills McCallum. The two first met in Paisley, while working for the same company, Robin & Houston, soapmakers in the Sneddon. John McCallum was born in 1847 in Paisley, where his father owned a successful dye -works. Young John was sent to the John Neilson Institution. After a good early education there, John attended Allan Glen's School in Glasgow, where he continued his studies in

Group of factory workers at Isdale McCallum Soap works, Paisley, proudly sitting behind the firm's famous advertising statuette.(circa 1910)

chemistry. After leaving school, he worked as a clerk and traveller for Robin & Houston, where he gained valuable commercial experience in the soap business.

Ralph Isdale was the practical man, who had gained his expertise working for various soap manufacturers in Paisley. McCallum had the "good commercial brain" of the partnership.

In 1869, the two friends began business for themselves in New Sneddon. Their new business, Isdale & McCallum, grew daily and soon their premises in the Sneddon became too small. In 1877, the firm moved to new, purpose-built works in Rowan Street, where the soapmakers art was exhibited in a new light. "Over all, the works appear to have the latest, up-to-date, well-equipped machinery, employing numerous staff, even in the slackest season". The firm even devised a new type of cutter, which could cut their prize-medal soap into bars, at the rate of 1000 an hour! By 1896, Isdale & McCallum, with other two Paisley soapmakers, produced in excess of 15 million lbs. of soap per annum!

With the business firmly established and now a household name, John McCallum took up other interests. In 1898, he entered the municipal life of Paisley, as a councillor and magistrate. At this time, he was dubbed "Honest John" by the locals. His nickname was appropriate, since in all his dealings in business or politics, "his life was honesty itself".

He took a deep interest in the church and was a staunch advocate of the Temperance Movement. He was a president of the Paisley YMCA and ran its

The firm's famous advertising statuette.

Bible class, to look after the religious welfare of young, working-class men. In local politics, he became one of the leading lights of the Paisley Liberal Party. "Always a ready debater, gentlemanly in manner and free from acerbity", he won the trust of the voters and was duly elected MP for Paisley, in 1906, with a large majority.

As a radical Liberal, McCallum was keen to extend the voting franchise to women and financially supported the West of Scotland Women's Suffrage Association. One of the banners the suffragettes carried on their marches was sponsored by McCallum. It read "Ye Maunna Tramp on the Scotch Thistle, Laddie". This was the trade mark of Isdale & McCallum which appeared on the base of the company advertising statuette. The statuette was often displayed in shop windows and showed an old man removing a thistle from a boy's foot. The boy's name was Alexander Cross. The original, much larger, marble statue was made for the 1888 Glasgow International Exhibition, to promote the company's new Thistle Toilet Soap. The statue was removed from the works in Rowan Street at their closure and now stands in Eglinton Country Park, Irvine.

"Honest John" McCallum held his Liberal seat for 14 years and received a knighthood. He died on 10th January, 1920.

ISDALE & M'CALLUM'S

SOAP.

Advert for Isdale McCallum's prize winning Thistle Soaps.

William Notman

William Notman
1826-1891

Photographer
Photographe

CANADA

38

William Notman portrayed on a commemorative Canadian postage stamp. His famous photograph, taken in 1858, shows the construction of the Victoria Bridge spanning the St Lawrence River at Montreal. (photo:courtesy Canada Post Corporation)

One of the world's great photographers, William Notman, was born in Paisley on the 8th March, 1826. He was the eldest of a family of seven children. His grandfather, William, had been a humble dairyman, cowfeeder and carter, catering for the profitable urban market of Paisley from his business in Causeyside. At holiday times, Notman's grand-father would take Paisley Buddies to their holiday destinations "doon the watter' in his covered caravan.

Notman's father had joined the swelling ranks of tradesmen and entrepreneurs of Paisley and began to make Paisley shawls. About 1840, with a downturn in this fashion trade, the Notmans moved to Glasgow, to become cloth wholesalers. For ten years this business flourished and the newly-prosperous family boasted a fashionable address in Glasgow. Indeed, when cholera struck the city in 1849, the family could afford to move out to a farm they had purchased at Stobhill.

Young William, as a member of such an affluent family, was given a solid, classical education. He became good at drawing and painting and yearned to become a professional artist. But it was not to be. His father persuaded him to join the family cloth business. During this time, young William had developed another interest, the burgeoning art of photography. At this stage, it was no more than a hobby.

It seemed that William would spend his life tied to the prosperous family business, but all this was to change in the fateful year of 1856, when young William would be declared a bankrupt and be involved in a financial scandal.

Like many wholesale enterprises, William Notman & Son carried a large extended debt and had problems with cash flow. Their principal supplier of cloth,

A typical high-class Notman portrait featuring, in this case, a young Duchess of Athol.

who was also their principal creditor, decided to supply cloth to the Notmans, only for definite orders. However, in a scheme to make money, young William continued to order twice the cloth needed. He then hoped to sell the surplus to pay off the family debt. For a while this ruse worked, but, eventually, William felt guilty and confessed his reckless business behaviour. He offered his household goods and all his assets to pay the debts to his supplier, but his plea failed and the suppliers took court action. To avoid the severe penalties for fraud and possibly debtor's prison, William decided to flee the country.

In the summer of 1856, William Notman ended up in Montreal, Canada. Always ambitious and with a compelling desire to succeed, he began work with a wholesale firm of dry goods merchants. So impressed were his employers with his business acumen and his talent as an amateur photographer, that, within a short time, they lent him money to set up his own portrait studio.

He was an immediate success and the elite of Montreal flocked to his studio. His portraits were of a fine quality, well -posed and finely-lit. Soon, his studio

In 1858, such was Notman's success with his photographs of the Prince of Wales during his visit to Montreal, that he was appointed photographer to Queen Victoria.

became the mecca for local artists, as he had opened an art gallery and exhibition hall. Always keeping up to date with the latest techniques, he was one of the first to employ magnesium flares in his studio work.

In 1858, his first large commission, which brought him international recognition, was to record the building of the Victoria Bridge over the St Lawrence River. The photographs featured Prince of Wales (later Edward V11) who had performed the opening ceremony in 1860. When Queen Victoria eventually saw Notman's superb work, she had no hesitation in bestowing on him the title "Photographer to

The back of a Notman carte- de -visite often showed the many medals his photography won at various international exhibitions.

the Queen". Notman had come a long way in a short time!

In 1862, with his reputation established, celebrities like Harriet Beecher Stowe (author of Uncle Tom's Cabin) and the poet Longfellow sat for him.

Branch studios were opened in Ottawa, Toronto, Halifax and St John's. Notman's gamble in going to Canada had made him a respectable Montreal man of affairs. He had turned his picture-taking hobby into a profitable profession.

His reputation reached America and studios were opened in Boston in 1866, to tap the lucrative Ivy League market. Wealthy university and college students would pose in group fraternities or at campus activities.

In 1876, William Notman was appointed official photographer to the Philadelphia Centennial Exhibition. This gave him the "exclusive concession" to take photographs at the World Fair. He exhibited his own work and walked off with the gold medal and high praise from an admiring American public. He also created photographic history by making the first photo -identity cards for the officials of the exhibition.

Further studio branches were opened in Hanover, Cambridge, Newhaven, Easton and New York. At the Hartford Studio in the mid 1880s, another 'first' for Notman was to take photographs for use by the advertising media.

The most celebrated portrait photograph in a long illustrious career was a double portrait of two sworn enemies Buffalo Bill and Sitting Bull. Other famous sitters were the actress Lilly Langtry and the author Robert Louis Stevenson.

William Notman died in 1891, leaving behind a legacy of some 400,000 images. His work is renowned in the history of portraiture. His striking landscapes of North America were innovative and memorable. Yet there is no memorial, not even a plaque, in Paisley to commemorate one of her great sons.

Paisley Cross

The artist James Elder Christie (1847- 1914)

In 1874, a large oil painting entitled "Paisley Cross 1868" was first exhibited in the town's School of Design, which was at that time situated in Gilmour Street. A few privileged Paisley gentlemen were allowed a private view of this newly completed painting. They gave it the highest praise. When the local press saw the work for the first time, excellent revues followed. One newspaper reported, "There is, in this piece of canvas, the condensed history of the town of Paisley.", while another described the work as "a most attractive and somewhat Hogarthian picture".

The young man who had painted the picture was James Elder Christie. Born in 1847 in Guardbridge, Fife, Christie had come to Paisley as a promising, young artist, to study at Paisley's School of Design. During his studies in Paisley, he became well-known as an artist. In 1868, he produced clever, political cartoons lampooning the candidates in the Paisley parliamentary elections.

At this time while staying in Paisley, Christie began painting a large picture of the town's leading citizens set against a background of the town cross. It was a huge project and, as Christie was leaving Paisley in 1874 to study in two of London's leading art schools, South Kensington and the Royal Academy, the painting remained unfinished. During his time in London, the 27 year old student continued his mammoth task and "after incessant labour brought his picture to completion".

The finished oil painting was brought from London to be displayed in Paisley. The leading citizens of the town were enthralled to see themselves represented on the canvas. They praised Christie for capturing their likenesses, which "were in general so accurate as to be in almost every instance easily recognised".

The artist had captured Paisley 'society', with its hierarchy of social groups. Most prominent are the mill owners, Sir Peter Coats and his brother Thomas, in the open carriage on the left. Sir Peter Coats is conversing with Mr Crum Ewing, Paisley's former MP. Mrs Jane Arthur of Barshaw stands in front of the carriage, carrying a parasol and wearing the most exquisite Paisley shawl. Not to be outdone, the two mill-owning Clark brothers, Stewart and George, appear in their private gig on the left. Christie's meticulous portraits included the provost, ex provosts, the town council, school board members and leading clergymen. The mounted horsemen in the background were the MP s for the burgh and county. The pecking order of Paisley society was clear in the painting's composition.

Noticeably confined to the shadows on the left of the painting are the town's worthies, Willie Love, Hungry Jamie, Daunie Weir, The Juck and the Charleston Puddock. When they were first spotted in the painting by some Paisley snob, these poor characters were decribed as "the more eccentric and less cultivated specimens of our community".

About eighty townspeople were represented in the painting. To help achieve a close likeness of his sitters, Christie took most of their photographs in his Paisley studio. As well as being a painter, Christie also advertised himself as a photographic artist whose speciality was portraiture.

The painting of Paisley Cross became so popular that the citizens of Paisley thought "the sale of the picture would be a matter of certainty and that it would not be allowed to leave Paisley". It was also suggested that the painting be photographed "in the durable process by Mr Christie, as a few would be desirous of obtaining copies".

Sir Peter Coats stepped forward and bought the picture and presented it to the town in 1898. A number of photographic copies were also made.

Christie's career in art blossomed from 1874 onwards. He gained a gold medal

Christie's masterpiece 'Paisley Cross 1868'.
The painting shows the leading society of Victorian Paisley.

in 1877 for historical painting. Following the current fashion, he lived in Paris for three years to study painting. In 1885, he returned to London where he became a founder member of the New English Art Club.

In 1893, Christie moved to Glasgow, where he associated with the new and exciting "Glasgow Boys" movement. Nine years later, he returned again to London and died there in 1914.

James Elder Christie had always felt that his roots lay in Paisley, the town which had given him his early patronage and requested that he be buried there. His grave lies at Woodside Cemetery under a magnificent carved tombstone. Today, Paisley Museum holds quite a few of his best works. These include a Tannahill portrait, some pictures illustrating Hallowe'en, Tam o' Shanter and, of course, Paisley Cross 1868.

Sir William Arrol

Sir William Arrol aged 36.

Paisley Buddies can be proud that one of the world's greatest engineers spent his formative years in our town. His name was William Arrol. He was born of humble parents in nearby Houston, in 1839. In 1850, the family moved to Paisley.

Young William began work in Coats' Mill as a 'cotton boy'. It was said that young William lied about his age to get the job! Soon, he was working in the mill turning-shop and sharing the work as a 'bobbin boy'. His fascination with the machinery he saw in the mills grew daily. In later years, when he became a director of J & P Coats, he fondly remembered his early links with the men and machinery of that great enterprise.

When William reached the age of fourteen, he became apprenticed to a Paisley blacksmith, Thomas Reid. Here, he learned the craft of working iron and steel from his master. As an apprentice, one of his more bizarre duties was to prepare the 'sheep's heid' for his master's dinner. This was done by singeing off the wool from the head, using a red hot poker!

As might have been expected of such a bright young man, William became known as a careful, meticulous operator in the blacksmith's shop. Everything he made or repaired was done with singular care and his services were much appreciated by the good people of Paisley. He held the monoply in mending cast-iron porridge pots and kitchen utensils in his spare time! From this, William managed to earn a few extra pennies. Once he had paid his poor parents his keep money, he had a few coppers to spare in his pocket. Most of this money was spent on lessons in reading, writing and arithmetic at night school. Often, he would buy some useful second-hand text books from a barrow in Paisley's Jail Square. He studied these and became familiar with the principles of mechanics, hydrostatics and engineering. Towards the end of his apprenticeship, he attended a night class in the shop of a Paisley weaver who taught boys mathematics. William excelled at this subject.

Having served his time, he began work in a shipyard in Renfrew. If he heard of any engineering innovations on the Clyde shipyards, William would trudge for miles to note and record it. In 1858, due to the trade recession in shipbuilding, he returned to Paisley and found work in Kerr's weaving factory, where his main duties were to keep the machinery in good repair. For his work as an engineer/blacksmith, he received 22 shillings a week.

When another recession put him out of work again, William enlisted as a volunteer in the 3rd Company of the "Renfrewshire Rifles". However, the only action he recalled was when his corps fired a "feu-de joie" in County Square, to celebrate the marriage of the Prince of Wales in 1863!

After a brief spell as a foreman at Laidlaw's Engineering Works in Glasgow, William set up his own business, in 1868, with a capital backing of £250. Despite initial set-backs, he managed to enlarge his works. He won the contract for building a series of bridges over the Water of Leith, to connect Edinburgh with Balerno. Following this success, he built his famous works at Dalmarnock, in 1872.

Three years later, his fame grew when his company built a bridge over the Clyde at Bothwell, for the North British Railway. In this, William showed flair and ingenuity, by constructing cantilevered girders on land, then rolling them out from pier to pier over the water. Two large bridges were to follow at Glasgow's Broomielaw. During this construction, he invented his famous, hydraulic rivetting-machine.

Between the years 1882-1887, he bravely contracted to build the second Tay Railway Bridge, to replace the one which had tragically collapsed. However, he reached the peak of his career when his company built one of the engineering wonders of the world and a national symbol of Scotland, the Forth Railway Bridge. For his work on the Tay and Forth Bridges, William Arrol was given a knighthood.

The Forth Railway Bridge-a masterpiece of Victorian engineering,
the eighth wonder of the world, built by Sir William Arrol.

Another of his renowned works was the building of Tower Bridge in London
and, by the end of the 19th Century, his firm had become the largest structural
engineering company in the country.

In later life, Sir William Arrol became the Liberal M. P. for South Ayrshire.
In this capacity he was once asked by a member of the House of Lords, "Are you
a civil engineer?". Always proud of his working-class background, Sir William
replied, "No, I'm a practical one!".

And practical he was. He always took a great interest in new-fangled machines
and financed the production of Arrol-Johnston motor cars from 1895 until his
death in 1913. Some important models built in the Paisley factory at Underwood
included the special snow tractors built for one of Shackleton's Antarctic
Expeditions.

Sir William Arrol was buried at Woodside Cemetery, Paisley, 'with every mark
of honour and respect'. On the day of the funeral, the town's flags flew at
half-mast for this great engineer, who was one of Scotland's most distinguished
sons.

Abercorn Football Club

From a Photograph by L. M'Lachlan, Paisley.

| J. Black. | A. Bates. | J. Brunker. | W. Fulton *(Captain).* | C. Smith. | T. Saunders *(Umpire).* |

J. Cockburn.   M. J. Drew.   A. M'Auley.   J. Fulton.

A. Inglis.   J. Goudie.

The earliest team photograph of Abercorn F.C. taken during season 1878-9. J.Goudie (front row right) as well as being capped for a Scotland v Ireland match also ran a successful plumber's business in Paisley.

In 1877, Paisley's first football match to be played to paying spectators took place at East-End Park. A large crowd of some five hundred people had gathered there to see Paisley's Abercorn Football Club play on their home ground against a select team of the 93rd Highlanders.

This regiment was at that time stationed in Paisley Barracks at Williamsburgh.

The team of 'kilties', dressed in full military uniform, marched on to the field as if in to battle. Just before the game began, the soldiers removed their tunics to reveal their kilts. The five hundred or so Buddies attending the game were somewhat surprised when they saw the kilts being worn for the duration of the game!

It was probable that the large crowd had turned out to see the 'sodgers' and not Abercorn F. C., as the club had not yet established a football reputation and this was one of their earliest games.

The three men responsible for the founding of Abercorn F. C. club appear in an early photograph. They were W. Fulton, captain, (back row, third from right), C. Smith, (back row, second from right), J. Goudie (front row, right). The team wear plain, crew-necked, wool jumpers and knickerbocker trousers. In contrast, the umpire, T. Saunders, wears a bowler hat, a three piece suit and sports the all important time piece in his waistcoat pocket. No designer sports gear here!

At this time, the line up in a game was usually six forwards, two half-backs, two backs and a goalkeeper. By 1879, Abercorn FC was well established with a good reputation in football circles and moved to a better ground at Blackstoun. There, in season 1888-89, they won the Renfrewshire Challenge Cup by beating their arch rivals St Mirren. Later in this season, they also beat another local team, the Dykebar Club, to lift the Paisley Charity Cup. Lifting the 'double' for the first time in one season was commemorated in the team photograph. Next season they won the double again, much to the chagrin of St Mirren. These were the golden years in the history of Abercorn FC.

The club was invited to become founder members of the Scottish League in 1890. That year they were heavily defeated by Cambuslang, as the Paisley team's full-backs failed to turn up for the game!

Other lesser-known local football teams around this time were Paisley Athletic, known as the "Zulus", The Paisley Olympic, (a pupil-teacher type club) and Dykebar. All these clubs were short lived.

Abercorn's decline began with relegation in 1893. Their support dwindled, while that of their rivals, St Mirren, still in the First Division, increased. It appeared that the town of Paisley could not support two football teams. St Mirren became the favourite.

Abercorn's swan song was in 1909 when they became champions of the Second Division. Due to lack of players during the Great War, the team dropped out of league football. The club had built up debts with the Scottish League from lack of income and support during the war. They had no permanent pitch. On occasion they played at Ralston Football Park, East Lane (now the site of a supermarket), but their glory days were over. The famous Paisley club finally kicked its last ball in season 1920-21.

From a Photograph by Turnbull & Sons, Glasgow.

J. Black (*Umpire*).   L. M'Taggart (*Treasurer*).   J. Haran (*President*).   J. S. Gemmell (*Secretary*).   A. M'Aulay (*Trainer*).
J. Johnston (*Captain*).   J. Heiton.   A Duff   J. Sharp.   D. Brodie.   J. M'Intyre.
R. M'Cormick.   R. Buchanan.   H. Raeside.   A. M'Lardie.   N. Munro.

Abercorn FC season 1888-89. Winners of the Paisley Charity Cup (right)
and Renfrewshire Challenge Cup (left).

East-End Park where Abercorn F.C. first kicked a football, way back in 1887.
This view taken in the 1950s looking towards Mill St. has all but disappeared.

117

Empire Music Hall

The grand opening of the Empire Music Hall, Moss St, in 1898. Dalno Fritz the new actor /manager and his wife pose at the entrance. A crowd of curious children gather round them. A lone policeman carefully surveys the scene from the background of Marshall's wine shop.

Johnnie Luske was a noted worthy in 19th Century Paisley. Although most people could write their own name, he could not. However, he could hold a reasonable conversation. As a lad, he had joined the "Dumbarton Fencibles", but he spent most of his working life in Paisley's flesh market. Long before Johnnie's time, in 1757, a flesh market had been built in Moss Street, nearly opposite School Wynd. In its day, it was described as "one of the neatest and most commodious of its kind in Britain", with "its genteel front of cut stone". It had been designed by Bailie John Whyte, who also drew plans for the High Church.

In 1835, when Johnnie Luske heard that the old flesh market had been bought by the Paisley merchants, Andrew and Ninian Crawford, and was shortly to be demolished, he broke down and cried, because he would lose his job. He could not understand why they should "ding doon the market, when it hae stood sae lang", but Luske was certainly no conservationist. The only thing he saved were the dregs from porter bottles, left over by prisoners at the nearby Tolbooth Jail! When challenged about this habit, he would reply that he was only saving "the wastrie that others had left"!

Despite the protests of Johnnie Luske, the old meal market was demolished. In its place, the Crawfords erected an elegant, two-storey, classical building which fronted Moss Street. The new building, with its tall windows on the first floor, was called "The Exchange Rooms". Situated near Paisley Cross and the business heart of the town, it was hoped this speculative venture would become the centre of monetary transactions. However, it was not to be and, only a few years later, the business failed. For a while, the building was used as "Assembly Rooms". In 1864, when times had improved, the building was converted into a concert hall and a singing salon. It catered for the many social soirees held in Paisley at that time and bore the grand name, "Theatre Royal".

As a general rule, theatres did not last long in Paisley, but, with a change of name or new management, things could improve. In 1896, the theatre was renamed "The Royal Empire Music Hall". Locals had another name for it, "The Rat Pit". It was here that the Paisley public first caught glimpse of the shimmering light of the cinematograph and saw 'Lumiere' type films flickering before their astonished eyes.

Once again, the theatre was given a change of name. Under the new lessee J.H. Savile and his new manager, Mr Habner, it re-opened as "The Empire Music Hall". The theatre was enlarged, re-arranged and embellished.

Two colourful characters who ran this theatre in its final years were Dalno Fritz and his wife who came from Germany. Dalno would stand underneath the gas lantern at the theatre entrance, dressed in a top hat, swallowtail evening coat, white scarf and white gloves shouting, "All pit and stalls this way!" Meanwhile, his wife would collect the money at the pit stalls. If any members of the Paisley public asked Dalno what the show that night was like, he would reply, "Terrible! Terrible! Go in and see for yourself". He would then tell prospective patrons how much money the evening's "terrible" acts had cost. This was a sure way to get Paisley punters through the theatre doorway! Once the house was full, Dalno Fritz would retreat to Marshall's wine -shop, next door.

Occasionally, he would perform his own sword-swallowing act. He would announce to his audience that he had not done this for a considerable time. His act usually brought the house down, as the audience expected an accident with such a hefty sword!

Behind the scenes, all was not well with his marriage. Dalno was a battered husband! The black eyes, inflicted by his wife, caused poor Dalno no end of embarassment among his male friends. His close friends, one of whom was a Caledonia Street bookie called 'Tiggy' Bonnar, banded together and bought him a one -way ticket to the USA. They saw him safely on board at Greenock and Dalno never returned to Paisley. Some years later, he sent his friends a theatrical poster which showed him as top of the bill at a famous American theatre.

Another notable act at this theatre was remembered by Peter Millar, who ran a butcher's shop in Love Street. He saw an act called "Mumming Birds". There was a young man performing slap -stick comedy as a drunken, well-dressed toff, who kept interrupting the other actors on the stage. His name was Charlie Chaplin.

The theatre, where the world's greatest comic played as a young man, closed in 1906. The building became a billiard salon, then a tearoom and is now an Indian restaurant.

Paisley. Moss Street.

This is the view looking down Moss Street in 1907. Horse-drawn transport appears everywhere. The fourth building in from the right, the Empire Music Hall had closed in 1906 and was turned into a billiard hall. Today the building is an Indian restaurant.

Burns Statue

Burns statue has just been unveiled by Lord Rosebery. On this day, 26th September 1896, a large crowd of well-dressed gentlemen gathered round to admire the splendid new statue.

Ever since Robert Burns had set the fashion in Scots poetry, Paisley had followed. The town has never been without its local bards, many of whom rose above the standard of mere versifiers. Robert Burns has always had a close following in Paisley. At one time, there were several Burns clubs in the town. However, only the Paisley Burns Club and the Alamo Burns Club have survived to the present day. The "Espedair" and "Thistle" clubs are consigned to the pages of local history.

Paisley was proud of Robert Burns. After all, had he not enshrined the town's famous weaving industry by giving the witch in "Tam O' Shanter" a cutty sark o' Paisley harn? In his love song, "The Gallant Weaver", the poet featured our town's river, "Where Cart rins rowin' to the sea."

In May 1896, several months before the Burns statue was unveiled, the eager Paisley public were given a preview in the press of the proposed statue. The picture, taken in the artist's studio in London, shows the statue model in all its fine details.

But to the folks of Paisley, pride was never enough. For a long time, the people of Paisley had wished to honour the bard in a more tangible form and it was thought that a statue in the town centre would be a fitting tribute. After all, the town had managed to erect fine, bronze statues in the abbey grounds to two disciples of Burns, Robert Tannahill and Alexander Wilson. The funds for these statues had been 'sung up' by the choirs of the famous Glen Concerts.

Between the years 1893-4, J.Roy Fraser led the famous Glen Concert Choir in performances of Burns songs. As the audiences were large, the funds realised were enough to pay for a statue of the poet. A Burns monument committee had been set up in 1893. It included a number of Paisley's distinguished gentlemen, all of whom were avid Burns enthusiasts.

In 1894, they secured the services of a distinguished London sculptor to design what turned out to be one of the world's great statues of the poet. The sculptor was Frederick W. Pomeroy R.A. His previous work was well-known in Paisley, for, in 1891, he had successfully completed a magnificent sculptured frieze to adorn the new County Buildings in St James Street. In chosing Pomeroy to make the new statue, Paisley would secure a work of art which would stand as a unique monument for all time.

There arose a thorny question. Where was the statue to be sited? Public debate was high in Paisley and letters flowed in to the local newspapers. Was the most fitting site to be at Paisley Cross, County Square or in the grounds of Paisley

J. Roy Fraser conducted the Tannahill choir at the unveiling ceremony.

Abbey? However, the council in their wisdom decided to relegate the fine statue to the Fountain Gardens. Some argued then and still argue to this day, that this was not an appropriate setting for such a unique work of art. Such a fine statue should be given a more prominent place in the town.

Despite all the controversy, large crowds of Burns enthusiasts gathered around the statue to witness the unveiling ceremony. This took place on 26th September, 1896. The proceedings began with the Tannahill Choir, led by J. Roy Fraser, singing Burns songs. The Ferguslie Brass Band accompanied the choir.

As the choir finished, Lord Rosebery stepped on to the platform erected around the base of the statue. He listened to Bailie Wilson give the story of how the statue had been funded. Lord Rosebery, who was an honorary burgess of Paisley, then spoke from the platform. "Paisley has determined to erect a statue to Burns, and, looking around at the many that already exist, has determined that hers should be unique. You at Paisley, then have a word photograph of the poet which will survive many statues". Amid loud cheering, His Lordship unveiled the statue which stood elegantly on a pedestal of red granite.

The choir conductor, J. Roy Fraser, then officially handed the statue over to the town council. He paid tribute to the "great host of working girls and men, who had yearly filled the ranks of the Tannahill Choir and who by their efforts had made the erection of the statue possible".

Provost Mackenzie then accepted the statue into the custody of the town council. He said of the statue," Paisley is now in the position of having a memorial to the national bard. Not only is the memorial a thing of beauty and an ornament to the town, but it affords the townspeople an opportunity of paying tribute to genius".

Perhaps in the future this fine statue, which has been copied throughout the world, should be given a more appropriate setting. The people of the town could enjoy this fine monument to our national bard and tourists to the town would love it!

The "Wee Co"

Samuel Connell who founded the first Co-operative shop in Renfrewshire, the Paisley Equitable.

To Paisley goes the honour of establishing the first Co-operative Society in Renfrewshire. It was founded in 1858 by a small group of weavers in the Charleston district. As a rule, the weavers of this district were self-reliant, independent, radical men, who fought for the working classes of the town. Some were noted for their intellectual culture, others for their technical skill, plain living and high thinking. When they gathered at the close mouth, they exchanged opinions and ideas ranging from politics to religion. Few subjects were overlooked.

Among the topics debated was the setting up of a co-operative to sell provisions. At this time, the condition of the weavers was not the most prosperous. The price of food was high, the town was still bankrupt and the shawl trade suffered from the vagaries of fashion, so weavers' wages were low. Also, manual labour was being replaced by the power loom, which meant some weavers were out of work.

Amidst this struggle for existence, a group of Charleston weavers met regularly in Stock Street. They discussed the advantages that a co-operative could bring to alleviate their scant family resources. They saw the social and economic salvation that collective trading could offer to them and their families. After a long debate, the matter was settled. To put their idea to the test, six of them formed the Charleston Mutual Friendly Society in 1858.

Samuel Connell was elected as the first president. Born and bred in Well Street, the son of a Paisley weaver, he moved to Charleston after his marriage. Such a move was almost like emigrating to a foreign country, as Charleston in those days was "out in the wilds" and had gained a bad reputation. Street fighting and family feuds were commonplace. Charleston was known as the "Republic" and was full of radical weavers. It was a common saying that "if you threw a brick in Charleston it would land on wan o'yer ain", so closely-knit was the community.

The society was founded in a weaver's shop at 37 Stock Street, Charleston. This small building on the right had living quarters on the ground floor, above, was the weaving shop. The small house on the left was the home of the society's founder Samuel Connell.

Samuel Connell and his wife set up home in a humble house at 36 Stock Street, where they lived happily until 1834, when the dreaded cholera visited Charleston. Sadly, Samuel's wife fell victim and died. While the epidemic raged, the scenes in Charleston were grim. One boy, seen playing marbles in the morning, was dead by nightfall. Each family suffered a loss. One funeral was a dreadful sight as it trundled through the village. The poor victim's body had been placed on an open cart covered only with a carpet and, to make matters worse, the carter in charge was drunk!

Charleston's reputation was still as bad in 1858, the year the co-operative's first shop opened in the back room of a weaver's house. Their trusted treasurer carried home the first day's takings, accompanied by a man armed with an open knife! On its handle these words of warning were inscribed "Don't give up the ship!"

The Charleston co-operative began with six members who each paid entry money of threepence. It was noted as a matter of some pride among the founding fathers that their first purchase was a quarter pound of tobacco. This greatly-prized purchase, costing fourteen pence, was duly shared and thoroughly enjoyed by the members!

Over the years, membership increased and so did the number of their shops.

At the corner of 9 Old Stock Street and Union Street (on right) the Wee Co opened their second grocer's shop. This small shop appears behind a gas lamp post. The adjoining buildings on both sides of the shop were used as boardrooms for the society.

From their early beginnings in Stock Street, shops appeared in Neilston Road and Duke Street. They sold bread, barley, peas, sugar and tea, butter and cheese, candles and, of course, tobacco! As business increased, so did the variety of goods for sale, including almonds, blue raisins and the "best mild-cured butter". In the South End of the town, well-designed butcher, baker and grocery shops made a welcome appearance.

In 1862, the Charleston Mutual Friendly Society became the Paisley Equitable Co-operative Society. This was to be fondly remembered in 20th century Paisley as the "Wee Co". Its big brother, the PCMS, would become "The Big Co".

In 1899, the largest undertaking of the Paisley Equitable took place in Great Hamilton Street, then known in Paisley as the 'dirty street'. New headquarters with a range of well-appointed shops on the ground floor were built. They included a bread room where fresh bread was made, a bread shop next door to sell it, a butcher's shop and a dairy department. Through a pend was a yard for delivery carts and stabling for horses. Above the shops, the society provided "superior housing accommodating over thirty families". Next to the shops, a large hall was built to supply a "long-felt want in the South End of the town". Over the years, the hall was used for soirees, Boys' Brigade and Band of Hope meetings, weddings and family gatherings. Generations of Buddies met their 'intendeds' at

The splendid headquarters of the Paisley Equitable Co-operative Society in Great Hamilton Street. The well-appointed hall became the rendezvous of young men and women looking for a 'lumber' at the 'Wee Co'dance hall in the 1950s.

the Wee Co dancing and it even served as a gymnasium for the old South School.

The Paisley Equitable is no more and Great Hamilton Street is no longer 'great'. It now only gives access to a public car park. Gone too is the often repeated question asked over the marble counters in the 'Wee Co', "Whit's yer dividend number?"

The emblem of the 'Wee Co' depicting a set of scales,
a handshake, a sheaf of corn and a beehive.

Paisley Town Hall

Paisley Town Hall viewed from a busy Paisley Cross in the early 1900s.

In matters of civic pride, Victorian Paisley was miles ahead of Glasgow. It had to be, to keep our big brother Glasgow in its place! In building a town hall, Paisley came first. Paisley chose an Irish architect to design her town hall, while Glasgow, some years later, employed a Paisley architect to design hers!

Until 1882, the year when our magnificent town hall was opened, Paisley had no hall large enough for the needs of the whole community. As far back as 1864, there was a proposal to build a large hall by public subscription, but, as the town was still bankrupt, this idea came to nothing.

In 1869, a similar proposal to build a hall in Moss Street opposite County Square was abandoned in favour of purchasing Saucel Hill as a public park. It was stated that the town could not afford two large financial commitments in one year!

In 1871, a site was chosen for a town hall opposite the museum, but, once again the budget failed and the project was abandoned.

Things finally got going a year later, when James Clark, with renewed vigour, put the idea of building a town hall before the public. Soon subscriptions poured in. Clark was so industrious, enthusiastic and persuasive that, week by week, a

Mrs James Clark of Ralston, who laid the foundation stone in October 1879.

torrent of money flowed in. By 8th March that year, funds had reached the grand total of £13, 870.

In 1873, Paisley received a windfall when the thread magnate, George Aitken Clark, died. In his will, Clark left the princely sum of £20,000 for the erection of a town hall in his native town. The building was to be erected in the Newtown of Paisley, Clark's birthplace. Combined with this hall, Clark stipulated that a large reading room should be built for working men, where they could sit in comfort and enjoy smoking! This room was to be kept open from 5am until 12 midnight.

All the subscribed money was returned when the Clark Family agreed to pay for the entire cost of the new building. The site beside the Abbey was purchased and a competition held for the best designs. In 1874, fifty -four designs were submitted. The winner was a local firm of architects, Rennison & Scott, but it was felt that their plans did not warrant erection.

Eventually, the designs of architect W. H. Lynn of Belfast prevailed, despite the additional costs involved. After an interview with the Clark Family, the architect was told "the matter of cost was not considered an obstacle"!

In 1878, work began on the site. To avoid noise and dust in the town centre, the stone, delivered by train, was cut in the goods yard of Gilmour Street Station. There, over a hundred masons worked constantly.

The foundation stone was laid on October 1879 by the donor's mother, Mrs Clark. As she was advanced in years and reluctant to encounter the gaze of a crowd, the guests attending the ceremony were restricted. Only a select eighty-two attended! Mrs Clark performed the ceremony without leaving her open-top barouche which was driven up a specially designed incline to the awaiting foundation stone. Provost Mackean, officiating, thanked Mrs Clark for this "kingly donation" and hoped that "the name of Clark may be ever green in our midst and their commercial enterprises be so successful, as to be at once a reward to themselves and a blessing to our population".

30th January 1882 was the day of the grand, official opening. The Provost proudly wore his new chain of office for the first time. A mile and a half long procession wound through the specially decorated streets of the town. 12,000 people, carrying banners, marched to the sound of instrumental music. People even came from exotic places like Shotts, Coatbridge and Glasgow to take part in the procession! The houses on the route were decorated in evergreens, flags and

George Aitken Clark of Newark, New Jersey, who left £20,000 in his will to build the Town Hall.

emblems. From windows, flags decorated with the words "Clark Hall" waved vigorously as the long procession passed by.

In the evening, a 'grand conversazione' for a thousand guests was held. The guests enjoyed a menu which included roast pheasant, oyster patties and Egyptian quails. And that was just for starters! A concert then followed.

At night, a display of fireworks from the High Church tower lit up Paisley's skyline. The town's public buildings and shops were illuminated by gaily coloured gas lamps. These, however, paled into insignificance beside the two large lamps in front of the new Town Hall, lit by the new electricity. They caused a sensation. People compared the space in front of the town hall to daylight!

The Town Hall, built, temple-like, in the Corinthian style to the East and Ionic style to the North was well appointed. The largest hall, complete with balcony, stage and organ could seat 2,000 people. Reading and smoking rooms for the working classes were situated on the South side. The South Minor hall could be used for various functions, including use as a masonic temple. Rooms abounded.

Two large towers reached skywards. The taller tower contained a clock, chimes and carillons, one for each day of the month. Two of the tunes played were Tannahill's "Bonnie Wood O' Craigielea" and, in the Radical Paisley tradition, "The Marseillaise". Each side of the clock tower was surmounted with statues of the Four Seasons, while the smaller tower simply acted as a ventilation shaft.

Over the years, our magnificent Town Hall has had many uses. It has seen Prime Ministers come and go, with men like Asquith, Lloyd George and Edward Heath facing the voters. It became a popular venue for Saturday night dances in the 40s and 50s, when Jimmy McCracken's band would play the night away. Talent competitions, concerts, boxing matches and pantomimes were also popular with Paisley folks. To have your wedding reception in the 'Art Galleries' of the Town Hall was considered very posh. And, who could forget the scenes on the balcony after St Mirren had won the Scottish Cup for the third time!

In recent years, our Town Hall has been renovated to ensure that this gift of the Clark Family will continue as an 'anchor' in the affairs of Paisley well into the next century.

The resplendent frontage of the Clark Town Hall built in the classical style.

The Town Hall with its elegant towers rises like a cliff from the banks of the Cart. Next to it appears St. James Bridge, which was re-modelled and widened to be in a style in keeping with the magnificent Town Hall.

A.F.Craig

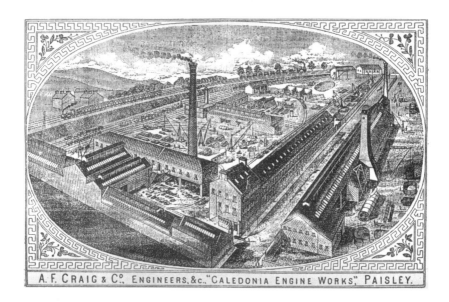

A. F. CRAIG & Cº. ENGINEERS,&c."CALEDONIA ENGINE WORKS". PAISLEY.

View of the Caledonia Engine Works of A.F. Craig in 1900.
A siding from the Caledonian Railway entered the spacious factory yard where twenty steam cranes handled the heavy machine products. From the factory an immense export trade was made to all parts of the world.

The Paisley firm A.F. Craig had a world-wide reputation for innovative engineering products. The founder of the firm was Archibald Fulton Craig. His earliest recollection was the removal of his family, of which he was the eldest son, from a tenement in Paisley to a house in the country. The unspoilt 'country' area of Paisley was no further than Gateside, on Renfrew Road. The Craig family had moved there to allow their father to be nearer his engineering works. The father, also Archibald, was chief partner in the firm Craig and Fullerton. His firm operated at the Vulcan Works on the corner of Hamilton Street and Renfrew Road.

Young Archie received his early education at two preparatory schools in Paisley, Galbraith's in Oakshaw and Reid's in School Wynd. He was then sent to Paisley Grammar in Oakshaw, where he won two prizes. He finished his education at a private boarding school in Kilwinning and was then apprenticed as an engineer in his father's works. After serving five years on the shop floor, young Archie was

The famous medal-winning, quadruple-cropping machine used by
leading cloth manufacturers throughout the world.

sent to America to widen his experience. During his stay there, he witnessed the
"terrible Civil War" drawing to a close and had the "melancholy satisfaction" of
viewing the body of the assassinated President Lincoln as it lay in state.

When he returned to Paisley, young Archie's next assignment was to go to
France as a salesman of the cropping machines invented by his uncle, James
Craig. This new-fangled machine shaved off the rough underside of cloth after it
left the loom. This had been a tedious, time-consuming operation when done by
hand. However, young Archie came back to Paisley with only two orders. The
machine was too advanced and complicated for the French to understand!

Archie decided to follow in his father's footsteps and go into business for
himself. For the next few years, he was busy building works at Macdowall St,
hoping to meet the anticipated demand at home and abroad for the cropping
machines and carpet power looms in which the Craig family specialised. By 1868,
the Caledonia Works at Macdowall St were established and the cropping
machines were selling well. Archie further refined the cropping machine design
by allowing it to crop both sides of the cloth at once. So successful was the new
machine that it won a medal at the Paris Exhibition of 1878. Orders flowed in to
Paisley.

A.F.Craig, his wife and their trusty chauffeur, Mr Cochran, stand beside Craig's gleaming Rolls-Royce.In their golden years, Mr and Mrs Craig spent many a happy holiday touring round Scotland in their Rolls-Royce.

At this time, the Caledonia Works at Paisley greatly expanded, with iron founding, general engineering and boiler-making being added to the firm's output.   By 1880, A.F. Craig became famous for making oil and petroleum distillation plant. They became associated with 'Paraffin Young', who founded the mineral oil trade in Scotland.

In 1897, Archie Craig went on a business trip to America to sell his cropping machines and carpet looms. One of his companions was Dr Archibald Barr, the Paisley genius who invented the rangefinder and was hoping to sell his invention to the U. S. Admiralty. During the business trip, the two 'Archies' from Paisley were introduced to one of the world's greatest inventors, Thomas Alva Edison. Archie Craig described him simply as 'the famous electrican' who gave them a conducted tour of his world famous laboratories. Craig recalled of Edison, "He appeared a much older man than I expected to see and he is very deaf, so that it was extremely difficult to carry on a conversation with him".

Meanwhile, at Paisley, the works continued to expand. In 1888, the firm "added greatly to their resources by acquiring the extensive foundry formerly conducted by Dundas S. Porteous". They could now handle the largest castings in

Scotland. They build sugar refineries, supplied Templetons and Stoddarts with carpet-weaving looms, produced iron roofs and bridges, spooling machinery, oil and gas plants, textile washing and drying machines, lifting cranes and boilers and vessels of all shapes and sizes. The list of their products was endless. A contemporary observer describing the works said, "The making of machinery by machinery at these works is a truly wonderful illustration of modern advancement in the mechanical arts".

Archibald Craig was now one of Paisley's wealthiest men. He gave generously to his native town. In 1915, he donated funds to restore the cloister walk at Paisley Abbey, where his family worshipped. In 1916, he donated a steam engine to Paisley Technical College at a critical time, when their finances were low. Archibald Craig was described by a fellow townsmen "as a man whose philanthropic sympathies and business character gave him a unique position in Paisley".

The company he founded gave valuable service to the country through two world wars and employed many Paisley people. The name of A. F. Craig & Co Ltd, was renowned throughout the world, until it finally closed in 1982. The age of heavy industry in Paisley and the Clydeside had run its course.

A huge, twelve-roller sugar cane crushing plant was just
one example of the complex machinery made in Paisley by A.F.Craig.

Charles Glasgow

Charles Glasgow, Paisley's famous coachbuilder, stands beside his model of the King's Semi -State Coach, completed in 1932 after three year's work.

At one time there was a Glasgow in the town of Paisley! This was Charles Glasgow, a dapper little business man who was a kenspeckle figure in Paisley for many years.

In late Victorian Paisley, he ran a business as painter, decorator and signwriter from his premises in Mill Street. He was no ordinary house painter, but specialised in high-class interior design and decoration. If there was a special function such as a birthday, a wedding anniversary or a society dinner, he was the man to decorate the rooms or halls. He advertised to his Paisley patrons the following;

"Mr Glasgow has had the honour of decorating for the leading Trades, Societies, Clubs and Church Soirees in Paisley and his efforts have received the praise of press and public". From his premises in Mill Street, customers could hire, for a moderate charge, flags and decorations for all occasions. Paisley had a plethora of clubs, trade incorporations and societies, which all held functions at different times of the year, so Charles Glasgow's business in providing decorations boomed.

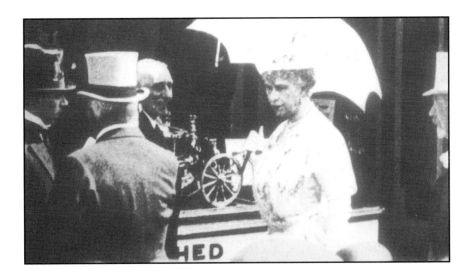

Charles Glasgow proudly stands beside his exhibition model of a state coach.
He has just been presented to King George V and Queen Mary.

To diversify his business, he opened a coach-building work in 1880, next to the old quarry (now East-End Park) at 18 Mill Street and kept the shop for his decorating business in Gauze Street. Initially, he specialised in making "Spring Vans" and horse-drawn lorries, again with great success.

Within a few years, he expanded once more and built new, larger premises called "The Reliance Carriage Works" at Smithhills Street. There, it was said, "In the modern economic history of Paisley, there is no more remarkable factor, than the rapid development of the artistic industry which Mr Charles Glasgow controls as coachbuilder. Through his technical knowledge, his well-directed enterprise, his excellence of the special classes of vehicles he produces, the works at Paisley have become the largest of its kind in Scotland".

Charles Glasgow's new purpose-built factory was four storeys high and was a showpiece of its kind. There was ample storage for the stock of highly matured, costly woods, such as ash, walnut, hickory and elm. An elegant showroom allowed customers to view the finished articles. The office was installed with the latest "telephonic communication", to cope with the firm's busy transactions at home and abroad. Adjoining this was the drawing office where Mr Glasgow would produce his own designs in full-sized detail. The smithy was lofty and spacious and was fitted out with three large hearths and the most up-to-date tools. The body, wheel and finishing shops were all equipped with the latest labour-saving devices. The varnish shop was cut off from the rest by glass partitions and maintained at a standard temperature.

Handbill advert 1880

Specially skilled artists were employed in the paint shop to decorate the vehicles. Top class upholsterers and harness-makers provided the finishing touches. A hoist connected the first three floors of the factory, so that vehicles could be brought to any part of the factory without difficulty.

From this state of the art factory, Charles Glasgow designed and built carriages of the highest class. He produced broughams, landaus, victorias, phaetons and pony traps and claimed the distinction of building the first hansom cab in the West of Scotland. He gained a world wide reputation for his "polo carts" and "inside cars" of which over a thousand were made. In 1892, his design for a hansom polo cart gained a gold medal at the Greenock International Exhibition. His "aesthetic brougham" became a great favourite with many distinguished families. One unusual commission was to design and build five gorgeously-decorated tableau wagons for the famous Transfield's Circus.

Charles Glasgow played his part in the evangelising of the British Empire by building "Bible Carts" for use in India. For the Maharajahs of this continent he also built special carriages and elephant palanquins. There was no end to this man's talent!

With the coming of the motor car, Glasgow turned to building motor bodies from his premises in Abbey Street, to which he had moved around the turn of the century.

In later life, he was presented to royalty at various exhibitions where they viewed and appreciated his meticulous models of carriages. In 1932, Charles Glasgow completed two models of State coaches after three year's work. He had spent many weeks at the Royal Mews, sketching, measuring and photographing the royal coaches.

He even made a limited number of Coronation Coach brooches, one of which is still worn proudly by a Paisley lady! Originally intended for the coronation of King Edward V111, the brooches were held over for the later crowning of King George V1 in 1937.

Cinderella would have been pleased to have known such a man! Some of his model coaches can be seen in Glasgow Transport Museum. Such an appropriate name would have amused this craftsman from Paisley!

Older readers will remember Glasgow's toy and pram shop which traded for many years in Cotton Street. There, carriages of a different kind could be bought from Charles Glasgow's daughter.

H.H. Asquith MP.

A political cartoon of H.H. Asquith dated 1924.
The wily old politician's favourite answer to an awkward question was "Wait and see!"

"Paisley has never faltered. I have called her the Maiden City of Scottish Liberalism". These were the words of thanks uttered by the Right Honorable H.H. Asquith to the Paisley electorate, who had just returned him as their Liberal MP in the Parliamentary by-election of 1920.

This celebrated by-election, "Paisley's Liberal Triumph", became the focus of the world's press. The election took place on 25th February 1920. The count of the votes, which was of national interest, took place in the County Buildings in St James Street. A crowd of 12,000 people had gathered outside the buildings in the early hours of the morning, to await the results of this important by-election.

St James Street had never seen the like. On the 25th February 1920. A crowd of twelve thousand people had gathered outside the County Buildings to await the results of this important by-election. When the victorious Asquith stood on the balcony of the County Buildings, the crowd went mad with excitement.

The crowds increased as it came nearer to the expected hour of the declaration, so much in fact that the whole of St James Street became congested. Fortunately, the three candidates had already made their way inside the building. Biggar, the Labour candidate, had arrived at 10pm, Asquith, his wife and daughter had arrived by car at 1-15 pm and the Conservative 's man, MacKean, at 1-25pm.

Inside, a host of pressmen stood waiting for the final count to be announced, before telephoning or telegraphing to every part of the kingdom. After a few false alarms which caused panic to the newspaper men, the correct results finally

When Asquith reached the Liberal Club Building fresh from his resounding victory, he was cheered and cheered as Paisley's new MP.

came through. Asquith, that old stalwart of the Liberal Party and ex-Prime Minister, had won by a majority of 2834 over his nearest opponent, the Labour man.

Paisley, always a Liberal sronghold, went mad with excitement. Great cheers echoed in St James Street as Asquith stood on the balcony of the County Buildings. From every house window on the street, men, women and children watched the large crowds cheering and waving the Liberal colours.

After a short speech in which he could barely be heard, Asquith made his way out of the buildings. When he reached the vestibule, he was showered by bags of pea flour by over-enthusiastic Liberal students, who had come down from Glasgow University especially for the occasion. As Asquith made his way into his chauffeur-driven car parked in St James Street, some more students attempted to hold up the car by tying a stout rope across its front bumper. When the car slowly moved off, the students tugged and tugged on the rope, until the car gathered speed and they abandoned the tug o' war. The students then clambered on board the car roof and running boards, only jumping off as the car sped towards Moss Street. This fiasco might well have been reported by the press as an act of hooliganism, until it was discovered that the students had only seized the car with the good intention of towing it up the High Street to the Liberal Club!

The Liberal Club had been packed out since one o' clock in the morning and, at 2-45pm, news reached the building that "Asquith was in". The news of the election victory had reached the Liberal Club in a most unusual manner. From a vantage point high in the club buildings in the High Street, a look-out spotted a white flag fluttering from a window near the County Buildings in St James Street. The white flag was not a flag of surrender, but of victory. The set-up had been pre-arranged by the enterprising Liberals of Paisley.

When Asquith arrived at the Liberal Club fresh from his resounding victory, he was cheered and cheered as Paisley's new MP. Sounds of "See the Conquering Hero Comes" and "For He's a Jolly Good Fellow" could be heard through the windows of the club. When his supporters' choruses had finally died down, Asquith made the customary thank you speech to all his fellow Liberals. His daughter, Lady Bonham-Carter, then spoke about how proud she was of her father regaining an office as MP. She said, "This not only means Member of Parliament, but Member for Paisley". This remark went down well with her Paisley audience!

After the early morning celebrations at the Liberal Club were over, Asquith held his next meeting that same evening at Paisley Town Hall. People queued in their thousands to hear the famous, old parliamentarian. When the doors opened at 6 pm, the Town Hall was packed out with 4000 people. The discomfort of overcrowding was forgotten due to the memorable nature of the occasion. During his election campaign, Asquith had made sixteen notable speeches in Paisley. His hour-long victory speech at the Town Hall was another example of his gifted oratory.

After his rousing speech, Asquith was presented with a medal. It had been donated by an old Paisley weaver, a former Radical. The accompanying letter explained that the medal had been originally struck in 1832 to mark the passing of the great Reform Bill. The weaver regarded Asquith's victory in the Paisley by-election as a new landmark in British politics.

With the election of Asquith, Paisley had returned the former Prime Minister to the scene of his past fame. Asquith went on to lead his party again between 1923 and 1926 . Today, this famous election is remembered in an old Paisley child's skipping rhyme:

"Vote for Asquith the man you know.

In to parliament, he should go.

If Mr Biggar says a word,

We'll hit him on the head,

With a horse's club!"

"Oor Willie" McCulloch

Paisley's very own "Oor Willie"McCulLoch

One Saturday afternoon on November, 1938, a meeting took place between two men at St Mirren's ground in Love Street. One was a keen supporter and St Mirren daft, the other the referee of that day's match. It was remarkable that the two Paisley men had the same name. They were not at all related, but each in their own way was famous. When Willie McCulloch met Willie McCulloch, it was said of their respective careers that one got the cheers, the other the jeers!

The man who got the cheers was Paisley's very own "Oor Willie". Willie McCulloch was renowned as an ace raconteur in the early days of the wireless and as a recording star in the early days of 'lo-fi', the decidely scratchy 78rpm gramophone records. A contemporary BBC broadcaster said of him, "I wish I had a guinea for every time I've announced that gentleman from Paisley over the radio. The person who can listen to a McCulloch character study and keep a straight face is dead from the neck up... or suffering from lock-jaw".

Willie McCulloch was born around 1885. He was of Highland descent, but lived in Paisley all his days. From an early age, elocution and theatricals were in his blood. Even at Sunday School and at Band of Hope meetings, he frequently performed recitatations and, at one time, became well-known for his Punch and Judy shows.

He received his education at the John Neilson Institution and then joined the staff of the local parish council. When he was appointed as collector of rates for the parish in 1916, he must have been the only such collector in Scotland who had a joke for every occasion. In his occupation as a collector of rates, Willie developed his ability to mimic the people with whom he came into contact, imitating their oddities and characteristics to perfection. This unusual talent formed his repertoire and he became known for 'leading other people's lives'.

"With his heart and soul", he entered the amateur stage. For some years, Willie was principal comedian with the Glasgow Orpheus Club. This in turn led to a

McCulloch appearing as Ko-Ko in a production of The Mikado in 1908.

long and active interest in the Paisley Masonic Opera and Dramatic Society. This local club put on several good Scottish musical plays and was among the first amateur groups to play Gilbert and Sullivan.

When the club faded out in 1908, some of the members, including McCulloch, formed the Paisley Musical and Operatic Society. In the new society's first year, McCulloch starred as Ko-Ko in the Mikado. For many years, he appeared in a number of leading comic roles. McCulloch also appeared in a memorable Glasgow theatre production of J.M.Barrie's "What Every Woman Knows".

In 1927, after serving as collector of rates for eleven years, McCulloch became a professional entertainer. Over the next twenty five years, the name of Willie McCulloch became known throughout the length and breadth of Scotland and throughout the world where Scots gathered. His audiences flocked to hear this pawky Scot telling funny stories in the true West of Scotland genre.

He soon became a frequent broadcaster on the radio, captivating listeners who thought his sketches so funny that they would "laugh until their sides were sore". As his reputation grew, he was engaged for concerts in London, Edinburgh, Glasgow and Belfast and given top billing! On the platform, McCulloch just stood looking as "serious as Job" and, without a twinkle in his eye, regaled his audience with his unique monologues. No one else could measure up to his style and standard and he was in demand everywhere as an after dinner speaker, at Burns suppers and Caledonian Nights.

Some of his most ardent fans included B.V. Lucas the editor of Punch, Alfred J. Munnings the celebrated artist and ex-president of the Royal Academy, H.V. Morton the essayist and many others.

McCulloch, "The master of voices", made his gramophone recordings at the Scotia Studios in Paisley. Most famous of them, recorded in 1947, was "When Agnes Got Married". This McCulloch gem begins... "The bride came in leaning heavily on her father's arm... tae steady him up! You know he's an awful man her father... not worthy of the glorious name he bears. He's called Drinkwater, but

McCulloch's later monologues were recorded on the Columbia label.

that's a libel on him... he disnae even know the taste o' it!" Other recorded gems were The Bluebell Chasers F. C., The Singing Lesson, The Chairman's Remarks, David and Goliath and Follow Follow, recorded after a Rangers win over Celtic in the 1928 Scottish Cup Final.

During his life, Willie McCulloch carved a niche for himself in the entertainment hall of fame. On 2nd February, 1960, he died at his home in Southfield Avenue, Paisley. He was mourned by a large circle of friends. Paisley has always been proud of Willie McCulloch. His pawky, evergreen humour remains as alive as the day it was first recorded and his original recordings are now sought-after collectors' items.

Anchor Recreation

In 1923 the Anchor Recreation Ground was opened. The jewel in the crown was the new pavilion. Local architects Abercrombie & Maitland adopted a Tudor design with half-timbered projecting gables supported on stone columns which formed deep set verandas at the top of the wide stairs.

In 1899, Meikleriggs was opened as a recreation ground, on a convenient meadow near to Ferguslie Mills. It provided facilities for tennis, cricket, bowls and football. On hot summer evenings, Coats' workers could be seen enjoying themselves after their day's work in the mill.

However, Clark's workers from the Anchor Mills, the other half of the world's largest thread mills, had no such luck! They had to content themselves with their only recreation area, a bowling green tucked in at the side of the Mile End Mill. The green had been provided by one of their directors, J.O.M. Clark, who showed a keen interest in the game of bowling. Mr Clark also presented the Oscar Clark Cup, for annual competition among Paisley clubs.

The lack of equality in the provision of sports grounds seems strange, as, by then, the two mills, Anchor and Ferguslie, were part of the same firm. Anchor workers even had to seek permission to tread on the hallowed turf of Meikleriggs.

A group of Anchor Mill girls, neatly dressed in hockey outfits, was one of the first groups to take advantage at the opening in 1923 of their splendid new sports field and pavilion. (photo:courtesy Paisley Museum)

All this was to change in 1923 and, at long last, the Anchor workers could 'cock a snook' at their friendly rivals, Ferguslie. Two large, open fields, which stretched between the River Cart and the Canal Railway, were transformed into a magnificent sports ground. Anchor Recreation ground was opened.

"Lucky Mill Workers" read the headlines in one local paper. Praise was heaped on Messr Clark & Co. for the benefit to their thousands of employees from such a bold enterprise. "Nowhere in Scotland, could be found its equal"! The twenty-acre piece of ground had been transformed, over a period of two years, into "an ideal sports ground". It had a first-rate cricket pitch, hockey pitches, putting greens, seven lawn tennis courts, a croquet green and a bowling green. The tastefully laid out grounds included a bandstand and an area set aside for an ornamental lake.

The jewel in the crown was the new pavilion. Local architects, Abercrombie and Maitland, adopted a Tudor design. The half-timbered, projecting gables were supported on stone columns, which formed deep-set verandahs at the top of the wide stairs. The dark-red tiled roof was surmounted by a clock with four dials. On the ground floor, nothing had been overlooked. It had a large cafe and two sets of changing rooms. The first floor boasted a large recreation hall which was lit from above and designed to hold dances. A series of smaller rooms, including quarters for the secretary of the new "Anchor Recreation Club" were amply provided.

Despite the bitter cold east wind which blew across the playing field on the afternoon of the opening ceremony, a large crowd of mill workers and their friends saw Mrs J.O.M. Clark ceremoniously unfurl the club flag and declare the grounds open. The first cricket match took place that day. Unfortunately the home team lost! Mill girls enthusiastically took part in three-legged races and sack races, to the amusement of the spectators. Music was played by the Anchor Pipe Band and the Royal Scottish Fusiliers, to the delight of the crowds. Two marquees dispensed tea to over 5000 visitors, during the afternoon and evening.

The day had been a great success and it could be enjoyed all over again, as the whole event, from the opening ceremony to the races, had been filmed. A few days later the film was shown to a packed house at the Palace Cinema in Paisley High Street. Mill girls clapped, cheered and laughed when they recognised themselves or their mates on the silver screen.

One year later, Anchor Cricket Club set wicket there. The teams played in the second division, twice winning the MacFarlane Cup and, in 1955, the Western District Cup. One popular event was the annual cricket match against players from St Mirren FC. Wee Paisley boys eagerly collected autographs from their football heroes, Deakin, Drinkwater, Lindsay and Lapsley as, bowled, stumped or run out, they returned to the pavilion. Anchor C.C. delivered their last ball in 1980.

The 'Rec', as it was affectionately known, became a social centre. Many a local youngster was encouraged to take up badminton, table tennis, fencing and snooker. Drama, piping, singing and a host of other interests was on the menu at the 'Rec'.

On Saturday nights, the building became a most respectable dance hall. Any hint of boozie breath denied entry to hopeful lads! One of the great 'Swinging Sixties' jazz bands to play here was the Clyde Valley Stompers.

Many Paisley schools, including South and Camphill, held their annual sports day at Anchor, with the pupils running in seemingly unending circles. Some secondary pupils, not the least interested in sport, easily 'dogged off' and escaped (as the author well remembers!)

Sports are still played today on five-aside football pitches and it is presently the home of Paisley Rugby Club, although, in recent years, part of the Anchor Recreation ground has become a private housing development. It is to be hoped that the remaining ground at Anchor will be preserved for the people of Paisley, like its old rival, Meikleriggs.

Robert Millar's Night of Terror

Robert Millar, who acted as official messenger boy to the AFS on the night he and his colleagues were nearly blown to pieces at Bell's Laundry. (photo:courtesy R. Millar)

In the dark days of gas masks, shrapnel and air-raid shelters, a young Paisley boy, Robert Millar, volunteered his services to fight Hitler on the home front. In 1939, just before the outbreak of war, he had been a keen member of Oldhall Boy Scouts. At the outbreak of war, Robert, like other local boys in youth organisations, was encouraged to take up voluntary service as part of the war effort. Boys could help out in either First Aid or the ARP (Air Raid Precautions) or join the AFS (Auxiliary Fire Service). Robert chose the latter.

After a period of instruction, he was posted to Bell's Laundry in Hawkhead Road as a messenger boy to the AFS unit based there. Robert's main duty in the event of an air raid in the area was to cycle as quickly as possible to his divisional HQ in Williamsburgh School and report on any fire damage caused by enemy bombing. Bell's Laundry was just one of the many strategic points in Paisley which held a two-wheeled fire-pump trailer. These trailers were called into action and drawn to the fires by commandeered private lorries.

The AFS at Bell's Laundry was commanded by leading fireman George Cassey. Whenever the air-raid siren sounded, George would say, "I can smell an air-raid tonight!" Robert and his older colleagues nicknamed him "Sirenitis"!

As the war with Germany intensified, young Robert spent most of his time with the AFS, working night shifts at the laundry. Initially, his unit were accommodated in part of the works canteen. However as the bombing raids over Britain increased, the unit was moved to a large air-raid shelter at the back of the laundry, where a full size snooker table and ample sleeping quarters kept the brigade contented during the long, dark nights. They even had their own swimming pool, a large tank reservoir of cold water! This was to be used to

The corner of Auchentorlie Quadrant and Seedhill Road today, with its modern shops built on the site where a Luftwaffe bomb destroyed a four-storey tenement in 1941, killing two people.

supply water to the fire pump in the event of the water mains being destroyed through enemy action. Robert's unit had adopted a dutiful, wee, stray terrier dog and called it "Plug". It was named after a piece of equipment to which the firemen attached their hoses.

The first sporadic Luftwaffe raids over Paisley began in earnest when bombs dropped near Amochrie Farm in Foxbar. The Gleniffer Braes were also bombed. (The Paisley Buddies had set up bonfires on the Braes to make the night-raiders believe they were hitting the town). At Dykebar Hill at the top of Hawkhead Road, the anti-aircraft gun had let loose on a Junkers 88 as it tried in vain to bomb the Rolls-Royce factory at Hillington. The war had come to Paisley.

On the evening of 13th March 1941, leading fireman George Cassey took his turn of fire-watching from the roof of the laundry. His prophetic words that he could "smell an air-raid" came true that night. From his high vantage point, Cassey could see the skies above Clydebank ablaze from the German Blitz. As he watched, Cassey shouted a running report to his men on the ground far below.

Suddenly, a bomb came hurtling down only fifty yards away from where Cassey had been standing. To seventeen year old Robert Millar, it was the most frightening night of his life. He would never forget the strange birling noise the bomb made as it came down, ending in a deafening thud. Cassey made a beeline from the laundry roof, raced down the fire-escape, ran across the tarmac and dived headfirst under the table in the air-raid shelter where his men were huddled together. After the initial panic was over, Cassey and his men believed that the bomb had not gone off. They thought that had it done so, it would doubtless have killed them all and taken half of nearby Seedhill Road with them. It was not until the following morning that it was discovered that the bomb had actually exploded. However, the damage was serious enough. The impact of the falling bomb had completely flattened a four-storey tenement at the corner of Seedhill Road and Auchentorlie Quadrant, sadly killing one woman and an off-duty policeman who had not gone to their shelter. The site, today now covered with modern shops, is an uneasy reminder of the grim realities of war.

That night George Cassey ordered his messenger boy, Robert, to go out on his bicycle and report "an UNEXPLODED bomb" to the Divisional HQ at East Lane. Fortunately for Robert, Hugh Williamson, an older member of the unit who took a paternal interest in the boy's safety, intervened and prevented him going out that night. Williamson thought that if the boy went out, flying shrapnel, which was everywhere, could well have ended his young life.

Two weeks after the Clydebank bombing, it was the turn of Greenock. This time, Robert's night shift was called out to go and help. Robert's unit requisitioned an old coal lorry, whose speed when towing the fire pump barely reached 20 mph. As they set out for Greenock, guess who was tailing them at the double? Their little pet dog Plug! No matter how hard the men tried to chase him back, stopping once or twice, he still faithfully followed all the way to Inchinnan. Plug was taken aboard and sat at the front of the lorry, as proud as punch.

By the time they arrived at Greenock at 4pm, it was too late to do much good. The town was an absolute scene of devastation. Robert returned to Paisley some two hours later and went straight back to work in his father's butcher shop in Love Street. For the young messenger boy, the war had only just begun. Robert went on to join the Royal Navy, serving out the full duration of the war as a leading signalman and surviving to tell the tale.

The insignia of the A.F.S. (Auxiliary Fire Service),
proudly worn by Robert Millar on his night of terror.

One of 'The Few'

Archibald McKellar DSO, DFC and Bar, Paisley's famous ace fighter pilot of WWII. He was small, fair, keen-eyed and witty. He bubbled over with good cheer. Once described as "the little Scots fighting man of the past, the Alan Breck build, with bonnet cocked against the world".

During the days of gas masks, shrapnel, baffle walls and bombs, the 'Battle of Britain' was raging over our skies. Several Paisley men were to distinguish themselves in this battle. Men such as Pinkerton, Howell and 'Doc' Allan, but none more so than the legendary air ace, Archibald McKellar DSO DFC and Bar.

Archie first saw the light of Paisley skies, in 1912, in a tenement at 4 Southpark Drive. He was the only son of John and Margaret McKellar. John, with his brother, ran a successful plasterer's business. The family moved to Glasgow when Archie was three years old. In Glasgow, young Archie attended Shawlands Academy. Although small for his age, he showed great promise on the sports field. His sharp eye, quick reflexes and excellent co-ordination would stand him in good stead in future battles.

Archie had two ambitions in life. One to be a plasterer like his father, the other to fly aeroplanes. The latter ambition met with stiff opposition from his parents, but Archie determined to fly at all costs. In 1936, he took flying lessons at the Scottish Flying Club in Renfrew, without his father's knowledge. Archie practised on Tiger Moths and soon gained his pilot's licence. The first thing he did to celebrate this achievement was to fly over his father's house in Glasgow, 'waggling the wings' of his Tiger Moth in triumph!

In 1937, he joined 602 City of Glasgow Squadron. For a man of his flying ability, it was relatively easy to gain his RAF wings. Besides, the RAF liked his style! He was the life and soul of the mess parties and excelled on the dance floor.

In 1939, when Flying Officer McKellar heard Prime Minister Chamberlain's fateful Sunday morning broadcast to the nation, declaring war on Germany, his reaction was typical. "Christ, I joined for the dancing, not for the fighting!"

When the first Spitfires were delivered to 602 Squadron, McKellar had found his ideal aircraft. He opened his account with the Luftwaffe in the company of that other Paisley pilot, George Pinkerton, in the first raid of the war over the River Forth.

A fortnight later, on 28th November, 1939, McKellar was first to sight a Heinkel over Dalkeith. He opened fire at close quarters. This was the first enemy aircraft of the war to be shot down over the British Mainland. Shortly after this historic event, photographers, newshounds and the government propaganda machine had a field day with McKellar. On the day, Archie appeared quite pleased with himself. He felt he had made up for his antics a fortnight previously when, after action over the River Forth, he'd rolled his Spitfire so low over the airfield, that he'd actually bent the wings!

Through the first winter of the war, McKellar refined his skills in preparation for the coming battle. Within a year, he would become famous in Fighter Command, winning the DSO and twice winning the DFC. On the express

The first Nazi raider shot down over British soil. This bullet-ridden Heinkel was despatched in a dog-fight by McKellar. The action took place over Dalkeith on 28th November 1939. McKellar claimed this as his first kill.

command of Prime Minister, Winston Churchill, he was given command of 605 Squadron, based at Drem during the dark days of the Battle of Britain. At Drem, McKellar was first introduced to his Hurricane fighter. Undaunted by its bulky appearance, he remarked, "No problem. I'll fly it standing up"! In an unforgettable show of solo aerobatics, he did just that. It was the master at work.

The action with his squadron over Newcastle resulted in '4 kills', '4 probables' and '3 damaged'. In August, McKellar received his first DFC for service with 602 and 605 Squadrons. Soon, 605 Squadron was moved closer to the action and was based at Croydon. Over a period of eight days, McKellar averaged one kill per day. News of his performance spread through Fighter Command, where he became known as "Killer McKellar". It came as no surprise when he was awarded a Bar to his DFC. The official citation read, "He is always in excellent spirit, is a particularly brilliant tactician and has led his squadron with skill and resource".

After action over Sevenoaks, McKellar returned to his base at Croydon in jubilant mood. He had destroyed four enemy planes in ten minutes. Ninety minutes later, he knocked out another fighter. Five enemy planes shot down on the same day was a record unequalled in two world wars.

His flying was brilliant, his marksmanship deadly, his reactions like lightning. This "Scourge of the Luftwaffe" had yet to have his Hurricane badly damaged. But time was running out for Archie McKellar. On the last day of October 1940 he had been mentioned in despatches by Air Chief Marshall Dowding. The day before, he had been awarded the DSO, for "his outstanding courage and determination" and for his "magnificent inspiration to fellow pilots". Tragically, McKellar did not survive to collect his medals. He was killed in a skirmish over Maidstone on 1st November, 1940.

Archie McKellar is now recognised as 'one of the few' of the Battle of Britain and as one of the most successful pilots of that battle. In Paisley, a commemorative plaque outside his birthplace simply says "Archibald McKellar, Battle of Britain Pilot. 1914-1940".

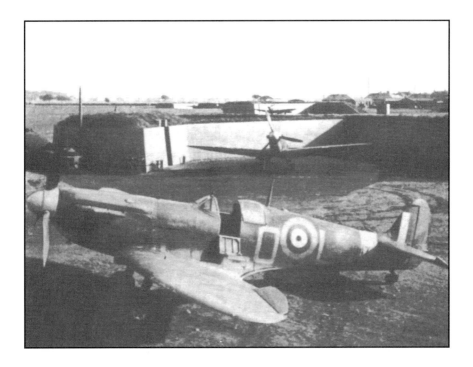

A Spitfire of 602 (City of Glasgow) Squadron. When Spitfires were delivered to 602 Squadron, McKellar found his ideal aircraft. In this revolutionary machine, McKellar's flying was brilliant, his marksmanship deadly, his reactions like lightning. (photo:courtesy 602 Squadron Museum)

Jimmy Cowan - a great goalie

Jimmy Cowan (1926- 1968).
A great Scottish goalkeeper.

One of Scotland's great football legends, Jimmy Cowan, was born in Paisley in 1926. He was brought up in the Cowan family home in Oakshaw Street, a pretty little house called Caversbank Cottage. The house still stands today.

As a young lad, Jimmy attended school at the John Neilson Institution at the other end of the street. When he made his way to school during the early 30s, Jimmy could always be seen kicking, bouncing and catching a 'tanner ba' (a small ball which cost sixpence) against the high garden walls which ran all the way along Oakshaw to the school.

It was obvious to all who saw Jimmy's skill with the ball that this young lad was 'fitba daft'. It came as no surprise when he joined the school football team as goalkeeper. When Jimmy was fourteen, he turned out as goalkeeper for the Renfrewshire Boy Scouts. Their opponents that day were the Renfrewshire Boys Brigade. It was a challenge match which was played at Love Street. One of the boys playing at centre-half for the Boy Scouts' team was seventeen-year old Robert Millar. Recalling this challenge match many years later, Robert said, "Unfortunately the scouts' ages were seventeen and under, while the Boys Brigade team were nearer twenty-one, which made the game slightly unfair!". The scouts were resoundingly beaten 6-0.

After the game, all the young players were entertained to tea by St Mirren FC. Jimmy Cowan, playing in goal for the scouts, was, at that time, so small that he could hardly reach the crossbar. However, Jimmy played such a brilliant game that he was singled out by St Mirren's chairman. The chairman likened some of Cowan's saves that night to the great Jerry Dawson, Rangers and Scotland goalkeeper. A St Mirren's Director asked who had been the wee lad in goal for the scouts. Cowan raised his hand and was congratulated on his skills. However, in typical Paisley fashion, the Director added, "I hope this praise doesn't swell your head." Young Jimmy was asked to leave his name and address with St Mirren.

When he turned fifteen, he played for his school team on Saturday mornings and, in the afternoon, for Sherwood United, a West of Scotland amateur league team. As Jimmy's footballing prowess grew, he joined Mossvale YMCA. Mossvale's team was considered the best amateur team in Paisley at that time and drew the attention of many football scouts.

In 1942, St Mirren FC signed Jimmy Cowan on an amateur form. One of his first games for St Mirren was against Rangers at Ibrox when he was just sixteen years old. Despite his heroic efforts in goal, St Mirren lost 5-0.

In 1943, to everyone's great surprise, Cowan signed for St Mirren's arch rivals, Greenock Morton. St Mirren had given him a free transfer! Nothing much was heard of Cowan until he turned out for the British Army of the Rhine in Germany at the end of the war. The army team beat the Scotland touring team 4-0. Cowan's goalkeeping skill at this match was a revelation. From this time onwards, he was capped 25 times as Scotland's goalkeeper, a remarkable record.

Few players are remembered especially for a single game, but Jimmy Cowan

Jimmy making a great save -
even for the photographer!

was. In the England versus Scotland match at Wembley in 1949, he gave a display of goalkeeping that has rarely been surpassed. The white shirts of England threw everything at Scotland. It seemed only a matter of time until England scored. In stepped Jimmy Cowan. He was heroic, he was brilliant, he was unbelievable! Shots and headers at Jimmy's goal did not matter, nothing escaped his clutches. The English forwards shook their heads in despair. Scotland won 3-1 which gave them the Triple Crown. After the game, Cowan was mobbed by the Scottish fans and carried shoulder high. Wembley had never seen the like!

Cowan stayed with Morton until 1953, when he signed for Sunderland for the then considerable fee of £ 8,000. Cowan was a remarkable goalkeeper. He even had his own unique way of working. Before a game commenced, he would draw a distinct line in the turf between the penalty spot and the goal line, with his heel. This enabled him to work out precise angles when he was off his goal line. He had been taught this technique by a great, old goalkeeper called Harry Rennie. When Cowan's team played away from home, this 'furrow' dug in the turf infuriated the home supporters, who shouted and whistled at him. Not surprisingly, he was eventually barred from this practice.

Jimmy Cowan was the one Scottish goalkeeper of whom the English media could find little fault, but his stay at Sunderland was short-lived. His brilliant football career came to an end when a boyhood injury to his leg flared up. He returned to Greenock, where he opened a public house. He died in Greenock in 1968.

Jimmy Cowan will always be remembered by those who were privileged to see him, especially for his celebrated exploits against England at Wembley Stadium in 1949. He was one of Paisley's greatest sportsmen.

Bibliography

Books:

The Paisley Shawl; The Paisley Thread : M. Blair

History of Paisley; Paisley Burns Club; Paisley Poets : R. Brown

From the Cottage to the Castle : Coats

A General Description of the Shire of Renfrew,1782 : Crawfurd &Semple

Judicial Records of Renfrewshire; Vanduara: W. Hector

Lanark & Renfrew : W. Hamilton

Paisley Abbey : A.R. Howell

Sanitation in Paisley : W. Kelso

Songs, Ballads and Fragments of R.Tannahill: A.Laing

Yesterday's Paisley; Recollections of Paisley;

Coal Flowers; Paisley Since the War : D. Malcolm

Abbey & Town of Paisley : C. Mackie

The poetical work's of Wm. Motherwell: J. McConechy

History of Paisley : W.M. Metcalfe

History of Paisley; Life & Opinions of Arthur Sneddon : J. Parkhill

Memoir of James Fillans: J.Paterson

Views in Renfrewshire : P.A. Ramsey

Paisley in Old Picture Postcards : V. Reilly

Pictorial History of Paisley ; Golden Threads : D. Rowand

Old Families and Olden Times in Paisley; Tannahill's Songs and Poems;

Paisley's Townhouse; St. Mirin;

History of the Lairds of Glenfield : D. Semple

Science & Gossip : A. Stewart

Magazines:

The Paisley Magazine 1828

Renfrewshire Magazine 1846-7

The Paisley Portfolio 1895

Seestu Magazine 1880

Newspapers:

Paisley Advertiser; Paisley Herald; Paisley Journal; Renfrewshire Independent;

Paisley Daily Express.

The Author

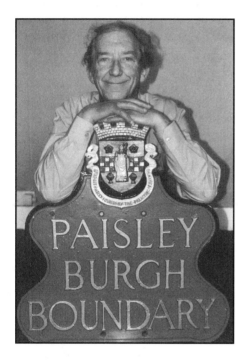

David Rowand is proud to be a Paisley Buddie. He has spent many years of his life on a personal crusade extolling the virtues of his native town......to anyone who will listen. His love of Paisley flows like the River Cart through the very heart of the town. Perhaps this love is inherited, since his Paisley forebears have lived and worked in Paisley since 1672. Rowan Street, in Paisley's South End, is called after an ancestor, Robert Rowan, well-known in his day as the Laird of Dovesland and Kilncroft.

His first book 'The Pictorial History of Paisley', published in 1993 is still a favourite with the Buddies. One writer reviewing the book for The Glasgow Herald said of the author, "He knows more about Paisley than there is to know." His second book 'Golden Threads' published in 1999, became an instant hit in the town.

In 1977, David was the moving force behind the founding of the Old Paisley Society and was its first president. Today, he is the president of the recently formed Renfrewshire Family History Society, secretary of the Bohemian Club and a keen member of the Tannahill-Macdonald Club. David was educated at Williamsburgh, South and Camphill schools, then studied architecture at Glasgow School of Art. He was elected a Fellow of The Society of Antiquaries of Scotland in 1980. In November 2000, David was awarded the distinction of being made a Fellow of the University of Paisley.